MW01181435

Relationship Rights (and wrongs)

A Guide to the Best Possible Relationship
and a Reality Check when it isn't

Beth Sampson with Melinda Wyant Jansen, M.S.

Checkpoint Publishing
Mequon, Wisconsin

Published by Checkpoint Publishing
10936 N. Port Washington #269
Mequon, WI 53092

Publisher's Cataloguing-in-Publication Data

Sampson, Beth

Relationship rights (and wrongs): a guide to the best possible relationship and a reality check when it isn't / by Beth Sampson with Melinda Wyant Jansen. --Mequon, WI: Checkpoint Publishing, 2004.

p. ; cm.
ISBN: 0-9722352-0-5

1. Man-woman relationships. 2. Interpersonal relations. 3. Couples. 4. Marriage. 5. Intimacy (Psychology). 6. Communication in marriage. I. Jansen, Melinda Wyant. II. Title.

HQ801 .S26 2004   2002113376
306.84--dc22   0405

Cover design assistance by Carol Reichelt
Interior design by Chad Miller/Fourteen Little Men, Inc.
Interior illustrations by Tom Price

Printed in the United States of America
08 07 06 05 04 • 5 4 3 2 1

What People Are Saying About Relationship Rights (and wrongs)

"I can now communicate with my husband. This book is a marriage saver."—*CP, married female*

"Thank you, thank you. This book gave me sanity. I finally understand why I felt as I did in my marriage, but I couldn't explain why."—*MG, divorced female*

"You give readers an ingenious and clear-cut way of evaluating their relationship."—*CC, female*

"This book helped me better understand and communicate with my wife."—*TM, married male*

"I never looked at my partner as a separate individual. *Relationship Rights (and wrongs)* gave me a whole new outlook on my relationship."—*PM, divorced male*

"Before I finished the first chapter, I understood our problems. My boyfriend and I didn't have the same meaning for a relationship." —*BT, unmarried female*

"The concept is great, especially the rating scales; the traffic light analogy is fun."—*GR, college student*

"It made me think about what benefits are really important to me, and what I need to work on myself. I found that I wasn't too supportive in some of my boyfriend's green rights."—*TR, unmarried female*

"This book sets a much needed standard for relationships. Without it I had nowhere to turn."—*BB, divorced female*

"The best book on relationships I've ever read. It should be on every home's book shelf."—*KS, married female*

"I tried to use numerous self-help books to fix my relationship, but the first thing they did was tell me to write a list. I didn't know where to begin. *Relationship Rights (and wrongs)* gave me the language."—*KS, married female*

"I thought your concept was so good that I gave it to my teenage daughter to read."—*EE, married female*

To the honor of all human beings in or out of relationships and to our families,
especially Jena, Judie, Harold,
Brittany, Ashley, Tyson, and Greg.

Thank you for the joy, enrichment, and respect you bring to our lives!

We love and adore you all!

What if you weren't feeling well and went to your doctor for a check up, but your doctor couldn't tell you the average range for a healthy body temperature, blood pressure or pulse rate? How would you know what to expect? And, how would you know how far you were from the healthy range or what to do to stay healthy?

What about your personal relationship? Do you know what to expect or not to expect in a healthy relationship?

RELATIONSHIP RIGHTS (and wrongs)

The Common Elements Found in Healthy, Mutually Supportive Relationships

A Relationship Guide to Use...

- ☐ for individuals in relationships
- ☐ for married couples
- ☐ for unmarried couples
- ☐ for people contemplating relationships
- ☐ for divorced individuals with questions
- ☐ for anyone who wants a checklist of elements found in most mutually supportive relationships
- ☐ for anyone who wants the language to communicate in their relationship
- ☐ for anyone who wants to get a grip on where they are in their relationship

Contents

PART TWO

Where Are You in Your Relationship? Your Relationship Reality Check

PART THREE

Additional Help—Help Yourself, Work with Your Partner, or Ask a Counselor

Love one another,
  but make not a bond of love:
Let it rather be a moving sea
  between the shores of your souls.

Fill each other's cup
  but drink not from one cup.
Give one another of your bread
  but eat not from the same loaf.

Sing and dance together and be joyous,
  but let each one of you be alone,
Even as the strings of a lute are alone
  though they quiver with the same music.

Give your hearts,
  but not into each other's keeping.
For only the hand of Life can contain your hearts.

And stand together
  yet not too near together:
For the pillars of the temple stand apart,
And the oak tree and the cypress grow not in each other's shadow.

Kahlil Gibran, The Prophet

Foreword

Do You Know What Makes a Good Marriage?

Most people marry at some time in their lives. Yet with so many people marrying, the makings of a good marriage still seem to be a mystery.

To most people marriage is a mystery enshrouded in a mixture of diverse emotions and behaviors. Musicians compose songs about it, poets write about it, and psychologists investigate it. It was sheer frustration, however, that brought two close friends, Beth and Melinda, to begin lengthy conversations about the questions in their own marriages. They sought to make sense of their baffling relationships and began to reflect on what specific qualities would identify a healthy relationship.

It was easy enough for the two women to describe some of the positive qualities they each wanted in a relationship, and some of the negative attributes they definitely did not want. But the territory in between the two extremes was so murky and difficult to understand that Beth embarked on an intensive study to find answers. She consulted with marriage counselors, clergy, friends, relatives, strangers, and even volunteered in domestic violence programs to get their perspectives on the riddle of close relationships. After gathering so much heady information, Beth compiled her observations for her own catharsis. She was able to synthesize these observations into a very simple and understandable format despite the complexity of relationships. Several marriage therapists aware of her work encouraged her to write this concept for therapists to see, as well as for the general public like herself. In time, Melinda joined forces with Beth, and so began the sifting, sorting, and editing of a mass of materials. Thus this book began to take shape.

Relationship Rights (and wrongs) is an illuminating reference book for relationships and is applicable to both genders. This important volume cleverly employs traffic lights as guideposts to help you assess the status of your partnership. Ironically, for years I've been walking around with imaginary traffic signals in my head, intuitively heeding the Greens, Yellows, and Reds that guide my life path. Go, Caution, and Stop represent distinctive messages that address the underpinnings of our most basic human rights.

I often find that partners tend to avoid honestly expressing their innermost feelings in the face of an uncomfortable confrontation. Often this is because couples don't have the language to be able to express themselves. They may look at each other tongue-tied or blurt out things they don't mean for lack of a better way to express themselves. This book gives couples the language to understand their relationships and express how they feel about them. It also will enable professionals to better understand and communicate with clients or patients. It gives relationship language to both the public and professionals. The concepts set forth in this book encourage you to express your heartfelt experiences in a readily accessible language that is easy to interpret. *Relationship Rights (and wrongs)* incorporates a wide range of examples, or "Reality Bites," to help you realistically acknowledge the most, and the least, that you might expect from your partnership.

Beth and Melinda, innovative pathfinders, have written a must-read book both for popular and professional audiences. It is groundbreaking in its simplicity and clarity. If you are just entering a relationship or working toward being recognized as having equal standing in an existing partnership, then be of good faith. With courage, you can look inward and evaluate not only your partner's behaviors but also your own in a meaningful way. As you think about and practice the ideas Beth and Melinda present, you will develop a better understanding of your partnership. As you do this meaningful work, your attitude is likely to shift and you might be empowered to effect a change in yourself or your relationship.

If you are wondering where your partnership is going, the many practical guidelines included in this valuable book can serve to inspire, instruct, and help you discover creative possibilities for reinventing a more loving and respectful union.

Lee Raffel, MSW
Licensed Marriage & Family Therapist
Co-Founder of School for Marriage™
Author of *Should I Stay or Go?*
How Controlled Separation Can Save Your Marriage

Human Beings Versus Genders

A GENDER-NEUTRAL DISCLAIMER

This book is about human beings and not genders. This book is about being treated like an individual in a relationship and nothing less, regardless of gender.

Neither gender has exclusivity on brain power, physical strength, creativity, cooking, earning ability, dishwashing, mowing the lawn, replacing light bulbs, repairing cars, babysitting, engineering skills, making beds, playing sports, reading a map, asking directions, financial prowess, cleaning the sink, legal expertise, raising children, or just about anything other than having babies. We're all human beings with the ability to do almost anything we set our minds to.

This book is not about stereotypes. Most people don't completely fit all of a stereotype—maybe some parts of it, but rarely completely. Each human being is unique with a special combination of qualities. All women are not stay-at-home mothers or nags. Not all men refuse to use a map or ask for directions. Not all women love to cook. Men are not always the breadwinners. Not all women love to clean the house. Not all men love to watch sports and repair cars. Our partners fall in love with the unique combination of human qualities in each of us. This book is about honoring the uniqueness in each of us and sharing it as a couple.

Since all individuals are unique, each relationship doesn't have to be 50/50, nor does it have to be 100 percent one way, 90/10, or 80/20. Each partner has different qualities that are stronger or weaker or of different importance. What is important is that both partners are respected as individuals, develop as individuals, and give to each other. One partner is not meant to do all the giving and the other all the taking. One partner doesn't have the right to hurt the other in order to get his or her way. Relationship rights are about empowering both partners to become the best they can be as a result of being in the relationship together.

This book was written by two women, but the genders used in definitions, explanations, or examples are not meant to be specific to any gender. He/she and his/her can just as easily be reversed in any part of the book.

PREFACE

IF RELATIONSHIPS ARE IMPORTANT, WHY AREN'T THERE GUIDELINES?

The relationship is over. Good, bad, or otherwise, it is finished.
But what really happened? What was I thinking?
What was I missing? What else could I have done?
I thought I tried everything. What was the problem?
Is there something I should have known?

Both of us—Beth and Melinda—asked these questions of ourselves when our relationships ended. In the process of trying to understand what happened, we had thousands of questions, a truckload of self-doubt, and not many answers. We rewound and fast-forwarded through our relationships, dissected them, analyzed them, and asked the same questions over and over again. Could we have improved them, saved them, or at least shortened the painful process?

In the midst of trying to make sense of it all, we read hundreds of books and articles. We were looking for a simple list of the qualities and behaviors found in healthy relationships. We also wanted a list of behaviors that should never be tolerated. Each book or article we read had its own set of answers and theories. Many overlapped, but no single book presented everything we were looking for in a complete, easily understandable, and readily usable form.

We Needed a Simple List of What to Expect (or Not Expect) in our Relationships

This book is the result of not only reading what experts said, but also using our own personal experiences, both good and bad. We talked to our friends, relatives, acquaintances, and favorite counselors. We observed other couples to see what made their relationships work. We even volunteered in a family abuse shelter to see whether such relationship guidelines existed there. From each of these experiences, we learned more about relationships and accumulated lists. It soon became apparent that if we wanted such a book, we would have to compile it ourselves. We certainly knew how it felt from the inside of our own relationships—both the good ones and the bad ones. We felt the need not to approach the book from an ivory tower expert viewpoint, but from a real standpoint as people who have been or are going through relationships—just like you.

In our process, we noticed that relationships qualities, we call them Relationship Rights, fall into three main categories that we associate with the colors of a traffic light.

- GREEN RIGHTS-YOUR PERSONAL RIGHTS: We call these your Green Rights because these are the qualities with which you were born; they should GO with you everywhere, whether you are in a relationship or single.
- YELLOW RIGHTS-YOUR BENEFIT RIGHTS: We call these your Yellow Rights because these are benefits you should gain from being in a relationship (or else you may as well be alone or living with a roommate); use CAUTION if you're not getting benefits.
- RED RIGHTS-YOUR SAFETY RIGHTS: We call these your Red Rights because these represent safety from hurtful behaviors that should STOP immediately; you have a right to be safe from harmful behaviors, whether physical, verbal, or emotional.

How This Book Can Help You

This book will help you answer three of the most often asked questions about relationships:

1. What should I expect?
2. What shouldn't I expect (or not tolerate)?
3. Is there more (can my relationship be improved)?

Sometimes in relationships it's hard to know for sure what to expect or not to expect, especially if you and your partner don't agree. However, in our research and experience, we found there were certain relationship elements in common among happy, respectful relationships. Based on this we identified twenty rights you should expect to have in your relationship in Your Personal Rights: Green rights category. Then we found twenty-one behaviors you should never have to tolerate from a partner in a relationship in Your Safety Rights: Red Rights category. And, finally, we list thirty-four benefits you can gain from being in a relationship in Your Benefit Rights: Yellow Rights category.

We include a measuring system that gives you the opportunity to check how strongly you feel your partner supports or denies each of the relationship rights. It gives you the tools to see if your relationship is enhancing or hurting you. Is the relationship a benefit or a boat anchor? Is your partner a cheerleader or a slave master? You now have the tools to determine where you are in your relationship.

This is a "Where Am I?" book, not a "How-To" book. Before you ask "how to" get somewhere, you first need to know "where you are." This book gives you checkpoints and the language to understand where you are. Once you understand and have the language, you can better communicate your feelings and issues to your partner, a family counselor, or anyone else. Your *Relationship Rights (and wrongs)* language and measurements can enhance your understanding of other books and strategies of your choice.

And finally, when relationship differences arise, it is natural for partners to fall back on the experiences of their family and culture, which might not be the same for each partner. This book will give you and your partner a common ground for discussions and assist both of you in transcending any differences in your backgrounds by giving you a separate, neutral outlook.

Relationship Rights (and wrongs) was written for anyone who is in, was in, or is contemplating a relationship. It is a reference source for the present and the future as well as for understanding the past. The information is organized, alphabetized, and easy to use, however and whenever you need it.

- It is a book for every couple's library, just as a dictionary or other family reference book.
- You can use the book for yourself, lend it to friends, or give it to young adults. It will help each person understand and establish appropriate expectations of behaviors in their relationships.
- You don't have to read the whole book. Once you understand your three types of Relationship Rights and how to measure them, we suggest you refer only to rights in question. Or, if you choose, you can read about all of them.
- You can take the time to measure and evaluate the impact of any Relationship Right that is especially important to you. We have even included suggestions for journaling.
- You can work on your rights by yourself, you can share this book with your partner, or you can take these rights and work with a counselor.
- The book is a tool for understanding relationships and giving readers the common language to communicate about their relationships.
- Once you know where you are in your relationship, you can use the "Resources and Referrals" and the "Suggested Reading" sections at the back of the book to find further help with your relationship.

This book supports all of these options.

We feel this book is a "must have" for all relationships because it is based on what it feels like when you are in a relationship. It is written by people like you, who are or have been in relationships. May you work through your relationships—past, present, and future—so they are happy ones.

Beth and Melinda

We Are All Raw Gems

WHEN CHILDREN ARE BORN, THEY ARE ALL RAW GEMS.

They need to be finely chiseled with careful understanding, love, and nurturing by their parents.

Neglect or lack of direction will leave them without any form.

Rigid obedience will leave them dull.

Arbitrary or severe yelling or punishment will leave them with sharp edges and large gouges that may need to be repaired or filled later in life.

Parents need to polish their gems with continuous strokes so that they can achieve their greatest brilliance. During the parents' time with them, they need to be cherished as the most precious things on earth, so they realize they are valuable solitaires and unique individuals.

When they become adults, these gems move on to be with their partners. Because partners enter relationships does not mean that their growth is complete or the gems are fully carved. While gems can shine on their own, a supportive partner can make them shine even more. It is up to the partner to continue to help develop and encourage the gem's worth and brilliance so it will shine to its full potential.

People have the ability to enhance others and make them shine like the Hope diamond with encouragement, support, and polishing.

Or they may quash them, dull them, reduce them, chip them, or shatter them into tiny pieces of sand to blow away in the wind as if they are nothing.

In relationships, we are all given the choice: do we treat each other like gems or like little pieces of sand?

Be careful. They are likely to become as we treat them.

Beth Sampson
December, 1992

PART ONE

THE MAP TO HAPPILY-EVER-AFTER

THE COMMON ELEMENTS FOUND IN MOST HEALTHY
& MUTUALLY SUPPORTIVE RELATIONSHIPS

Our Stories

Beth's Story

Just like most people—and probably even like you—I was in a marriage trying to make it work.

I am not an author, a family therapist, or a therapist of any kind, only a person who believed in a loving relationship and a commitment to marriage—as did my husband. I was well educated with a B.A. in economics from Newcomb College of Tulane University, and attended Columbia University for my M.B.A. in 1969 (before Title IX). I was willing to give up my career when I married, but I was always able to work and contribute a good income to the family. My husband and I loved each other and were always faithful to each other. We came from homes where neither side was divorced, and we believed our parents were good role models for marriage. We seemed to have a solid background to build from. We dated for almost two years before marrying. When we married, I was twenty-nine and my husband was thirty-three; it was the first marriage for both of us. So being married too young or changing when we "grew up" was not an issue. We had no "ex's" to fight, no stepkids to juggle. We were financially stable and neither of us used drugs or alcohol. We had every reason to believe our marriage would work.

But from the beginning, as soon as I said, "I do," I could tell the relationship had changed overnight. It became even more obvious when the honeymoon was over. I thought that if I worked harder, did things better, or gave up more of myself that our relationship would go back to the mutually supportive one I had known before we were married. However, nothing seemed to work so we tried marriage counseling and more marriage counseling and even more marriage counseling after that. In total, we were in and out of different kinds of marriage counseling for eighteen of the twenty years we were married. We tried secular counselors, religious counselors, and lay counselors. We tried counselors who were men, women, and even a man and a woman together. There were sessions alone, together, and my husband was in a men's group. We were willing to do whatever the counselors told us to do in order to fix the marriage. But none of the highly recommended marriage counseling programs were able to identify or fix the problems, even with all our years of trying. After it was all over, I wondered, "If counselors couldn't help a loving couple who wanted to make their marriage work, where both partners were willing to go to counseling and work at it, what would happen to really tough relationships?" What went wrong? What should we have known? What should have been done differently to either fix the marriage or get out sooner? So began my journey as an author.

What were the counselors thinking all those years when we were going to them saying that something was wrong? What should I have known as a partner and what could I have done differently to have prevented this, fixed the relationship, and helped us understand, or at least cut off the marriage sooner? My husband, my daughter, and I were all victims of the process. I wanted a simple list of what to expect or not to expect in a healthy, mutually supportive relationship.

So I took several years to research and find this list, including reading, and using my own life experiences and those of other people as well as volunteering in a domestic abuse shelter. The result of the search was my personal catharsis from twenty years of marriage. I compiled a list of the common elements found in healthy, mutually supportive relationships and a simple way to understand and communicate them. This is what I needed as a partner for the twenty years we were married, the eighteen years we were in and out of marriage counseling, and even when the marriage was over. It would have given our relationship direction and mutual agreement of how to treat each other (without turning to prior expectations), understanding of where we were in our relationship as individuals (both positive and negative), language to clearly communicate between partners (with independent neutral definitions), and a method to explain how we were treating each other with common meaning. The concept was based on:

1) a mutual starting agreement in a relationship, that "both partners are individual human beings and deserve to be treated that way"

2) a list and definitions of the elements found in most healthy, mutually supportive relationships to help people understand and communicate about what they have or don't have in their own relationship

3) a measuring scale to see where you are in your relationship based on how strongly you feel the elements are supported or denied toward you as an individual as stated in the starting agreement

When I shared the concept with some different marriage counselors, they urged me to write articles or a book about it. They initially asked me to write the book for marriage counselors or professionals so that they could better understand the needs of a partner in a troubled relationship. However, *Relationship Rights (and wrongs)* is for people in relationships or contemplating relationships, as well as for professionals to use in therapy.

Melinda Wyant Jansen and I have known each other for eighteen years, throughout good and bad relationship times. As the book took form, she and I collaborated, combining our inputs, experiences, and shared research.

Relationship Rights (and wrongs) is written from the standpoint of a "regular" person within a relationship. It is not written based on the views of a specialist on the outside of a relationship looking in. It doesn't assume regular people have the same knowledge about relationships as professionals or the language to appropriately express themselves to either their partner or professionals. (Obviously, if we all knew what to expect of each other and had the ability to clearly communicate it, we wouldn't be having so many relationship problems.)

So the book is written to give partners a guideline of the common elements found in healthy, mutually supportive relationships. This guideline gives partners an easy-to-use list of healthy elements so that partners have a simple way to see what they have or don't have in their own relationship compared to these healthy, mutual relationships. They can measure, understand, and communicate where they are in their own relationship based on how they feel these elements are supported, denied, or controlled.

Note: this may be very different than a compatible relationship, because a compatible relationship doesn't necessarily have to be healthy for both individuals in it. A compatible relationship just means two people can co-exist together, but they both don't have to thrive and grow as individuals.

As mentioned before, this is a "Where-Am-I?" book, not a "How-To" book. It is a resource book for all relationships, not one based on gender stereotypes for relationship roles.

I hope that the simplicity of the concept and understanding each partner's three types of Relationship Rights will help you as much as it did me. If I can help one other person or child from going through what we did, then I will feel that I have succeeded. Please let me know...Beth

Melinda's Story

When Beth and I met in 1986, I was a newly divorced single mom reeling from my second failed marriage—this time with three small children. One of my neverending activities was analyzing and reanalyzing my relationships so that I would not make the same "mistakes" again. Many Saturday mornings were spent over coffee with Beth, trying to clear the fog only to telephone later to share an "ah-ha" moment—when the fog cleared and the lights went on. But it was not until many years later when Beth was newly divorced and the idea of a relationship traffic light started flashing in her head that I began to have any clarity or understanding about my own relationships. The concepts and lists that grew out of her brainchild ultimately provided us with the language we had both been searching for. What you are about to encounter in this book is simple yet rich with depth and meaning and it is applicable to many relationship contexts. As a counselor working primarily with children, teens, and families in a school setting, I utilize the ideas and language set forth in this book every day. My hope is that this book will initiate an "ah-ha" moment for you, the reader, and that our years of work will help you learn about the inner workings of your relationship so that it can become all that you deserve it to be...Melinda

Chapter One

SO YOU'RE IN A RELATIONSHIP . . .

Where Are You and Where Do You Want to Go?

Most of us enter a relationship without a clear understanding of what rights we, as individuals, should have in the relationship. If we are not exactly sure of our rights in a relationship, we have no way to identify, measure, or evaluate them. We know only what we were taught by our families and cultures—and, much to our surprise, those teachings might not have been the same for our partners. Both partners need to have the same road map or guidelines for a relationship to succeed. If you are like us, you and your partner had a fairly well-developed set of beliefs about relationships long before you ever met each other.

Most of us have dreams about fairy-tale relationships lasting forever. The Fair Princess and the Charming Prince ride off into the sunset on a great white stallion and live happily ever after. Certainly we realize that the horse might stumble a little, or the prince and the princess might periodically get lost along the way— but still we expect most of the trip to be pleasant and ultimately head toward *Happily-Ever-After* rather than *NeverNeverland*.

When we suddenly face other outcomes, we are confused. Where are we? Where did *Happily-Ever-After* go? Did anyone ever tell you that instead of riding into the sunset to *Happily-Ever-After* you might end up someplace else? When you dreamed of your fairy-tale relationship with your partner, did you ever think the following scenarios could happen?

a) The mighty stallion falls, breaks his two front legs, and has to be shot. Your partner then walks off, leaves you alone, and comes back only at night to sleep.

   When you sound confused or hurt, your partner responds by saying to you, "What's the matter? This is the way it is supposed to be."

b) Your partner drops the horse's reins, and you keep going around in circles. Sometimes things get better, but then the same problems, or worse ones, return.

   When you sound confused or hurt, your partner says, "What's the matter? I know what I am doing; this is where we are supposed to be."

c) Your big beautiful stallion gets frightened and throws you off, and you land in a pile of horse manure. As you try to dig your way out, your partner keeps shoveling more on you.

   When you sound confused or hurt, your partner sees you covered with manure desperately trying to get out of the manure pile, and says with a smile, "What's the matter? You're supposed to like this."

Do you feel good about where you are in your relationship or do you feel confused? Do you feel you are in any of these other circumstances rather than on your way to *Happily-Ever-After*? In many relationships, the partners do live happily ever after. They learn how to survive the pitfalls and work together to solve their problems. So, the question isn't "Where do you think you are going with your partner?" but rather "Where are you now?" Are you riding on the white stallion, or are you walking behind your partner and the horse? And finally, a key question to ask is, "Where are you finding yourself instead?" We are not prepared for the destinations of a), b), or c). When we arrive at them, we try to use our old beliefs to guide us back to *Happily-Ever-After*, but we discover we're not sure where we are or what's true and what's false. Our old beliefs might not work in this new relationship environment.

FACT OR FICTION . . . WHAT BELIEFS DID YOU BRING TO YOUR RELATIONSHIP?

Unfortunately, over the past generations many people have been taught to accept fiction rather than fact, to believe that one partner should control the other, or to assume the blame for a failed relationship, even when it is personally hurtful. From preschoolers to teenagers to adults, people are taught healthy and unhealthy beliefs and expectations about relationships. Many of us enter relationships with dangerous generalizations, irrational beliefs, and unrealistic expectations that get us into trouble long before the "I dos" are even uttered!

What do you really believe about relationships? What does your partner tell you to believe? Take a few minutes to think about the relationship expectations and beliefs you brought to your current relationship. Then rate each of the below statements true or false.

TRUE OR FALSE

Mark each statement with a **T** for true or an **F** for false, based on what you were taught or believe about relationships.

1. ___ I can make my relationship work if I just try a little harder.

2. ___ I must disregard my own feelings for the sake of the relationship.

3. ___ Being in a lasting relationship is the ultimate goal in life.

4. ___ My partner and I should become one.

5. ___ Only one person can be the head of a household.

6. ___ If someone chooses me as a relationship partner, my life is a success.

7. ___ My partner should make me complete.

8. ___ A relationship will work as long as men and women maintain their roles.

9. ___ Both partners are to blame in a bad relationship.

10. ___ Being in a relationship is a sign of success (or popularity). Being alone is a sign of rejection or being unlikable.

11. ___ Disagreements are destructive to a relationship and are a sign of trouble.

12. ___ The grass isn't greener on the other side of the relationship fence. Even if I leave this relationship, the next one will be the same, so I should just tolerate it.

13. ___ I can make my partner change if I am good.

14. ___ My relationship isn't great, but it's okay, so I shouldn't ask for more.

15. ___ All decisions in a relationship must be mutual.

16. ___ If I make a mistake, I deserve to be punished by my partner.

17. ___ I should do or give up whatever is necessary to keep the relationship together.

How many statements did you mark "T"___, and how many did you mark "F"___?

FACT OR FICTION?

Now for each of the above statements you marked "T," look at the same statement below coupled with an alternative belief. For each of the statements you are reviewing, mark which belief you prefer in each pair for your own relationship.

1a. ___ I can make my relationship work if I just try a little harder.

b. ___ *It is not just one partner's responsibility to keep the relationship together.*

2a. ___ I must disregard my own feelings for the sake of the relationship.

b. ___ *I have feelings in the relationship, and they are as important as those of my partner.*

3a. ___ Being in a lasting relationship is the ultimate goal in life.

b. ___ *A lasting relationship is not my final destination in life. The relationship should also enhance me as an individual (or else I might as well live with a roommate or stay single).*

4a. ___ My partner and I should become one.

b. ___ *Being in a relationship does not mean I have to stop being an individual with separate thoughts and feelings. It just means that my partner and I have more opportunities to grow and share together as one relationship.*

5a. ___ Only one person can be the head of a household.

b. ___ *A healthy relationship is not a contract for one partner to control the other. It is a partnership of mutual respect and development.*

6a. ___ If someone chooses me as a relationship partner, my life is a success.

b. ___ *Simply being in a relationship is not a sign of popularity or success in life. While in a relationship, I still need to be respected and treated like an individual.*

7a. ___ My partner should make me complete.

b. ___ *Both partners are unique whole individuals before entering a relationship. The relationship should just enhance what they already are.*

8a. ___ A relationship will work as long as men and women maintain their roles.

b. ___ *A relationship is not made of men and women filling stereotypical roles. It is made of two unique individuals fulfilling their own personal needs and potential.*

9a. ___ Both partners are to blame in a bad relationship.

b. ___ *Relationship problems are not always two-sided.*

10a. ___ Being in a relationship is a sign of success (or popularity). Being alone is a sign of rejection or being unlikable.

b. ___ *I do not need a relationship to keep me company. I like myself for who I am and am happy with my individuality. I would rather be happy and alone than treated badly in a relationship.*

11a. ___ Disagreements are destructive to a relationship and are a sign of trouble.

b. ___ *Disagreements are a normal part of any relationship and are healthy when handled in a positive and respectful way.*

12a. ___ The grass isn't greener on the other side of the relationship fence. Even if I leave this relationship, the next one will be the same, so I should just tolerate it.

b. ___ *Just because this relationship doesn't seem to be working or has already failed doesn't mean the same thing will happen in another relationship with a different partner.*

13a. ___ I can make my partner change if I am good.

b. ___ *I cannot change my partner. My partner has to choose to change himself or herself.*

14a. ___ My relationship isn't great, but it's okay, so I shouldn't ask for more.

b. ___ *Even though my relationship is okay, that doesn't mean I shouldn't want to improve it.*

15a. ___ All decisions in a relationship must be mutual.

b. ___ *Both partners in a relationship have intelligence and deserve reasonable parameters and respect to make decisions on their own without being judged.*

16a. ___ If I make a mistake, I deserve to be punished by my partner.

b. ___ *Everyone makes mistakes sometimes. Mistakes are a natural part of life. No partner is a better person than the other, giving them the right to punish the other.*

17a. ___ I should do or give up whatever is necessary to keep the relationship together.

b. ___ *If my partner loves and respects me for who I am, I shouldn't be expected to stop being myself or to give up family, friends, or interests to please him or her. I shouldn't be expected to live in fear of my partner's judgments or threats in order to maintain the relationship. If I must live that way, then my relationship is diminishing me, not enhancing me.*

Have your answers changed at all from the first true or false list? Circle the pairs of statements that have changed. Read below to understand the differences.

FACT OR FICTION QUIZ RESULTS

First Statements in Each Pair:

These are beliefs that many of us might have grown up with and could have been taught as "facts." When we hear these statements by themselves, they sound logical and irrefutable. They are also statements that you may use to justify staying in a relationship at any expense to yourself. Your partner might also use these statements to justify his or her actions toward you. These statements might confuse you because at face value they sound so true and you may have believed them for a long time.

The truth is, these beliefs don't support the individuality and development of both partners in a relationship. The statements can be used to support the control and mistreatment of partners and to justify bad behaviors. Statements such as these can cause hurt, diminishment, and confusion in relationships that are meant to provide enhancement, respect, and support. If you are living with many of these beliefs, either from your past or from your partner, you should stand up for mutual respect and rethink your relationship goals.

Second Statements in Each Pair:

These are beliefs that are grounded in mutual respect for both partners. They set healthy standards and serve to enhance both partners' lives rather than serving just one. There is give and take in all healthy relationships, and these statements support that mutuality.

If you agree with most of the second "b" statements, you have a good foundation for a healthy and satisfying relationship. Both partners are supportive and accepting of each other. Your relationship helps each of you reach your full potential and share the joys of each other's lives.

Now ask yourself, how do you think your partner would answer each pair of questions? Do you think they match with yours? How does this make you feel?

So Where Is Happily-Ever-After?

It does exist, but it's not perfect; perfection is an unrealistic expectation. In *Happily-Ever-After* differences exist, problems occur, and there are crises to handle. However, this is a place where couples know how to handle situations like these together with respect for each other. They encourage and support each other, as well as apologize and forgive each other when mistakes happen. They enjoy being together and care about how the other feels. They are able to grow as individuals to fulfill their potential and share together. They make each other better individuals and the relationship grows stronger.

The rest of this book will help you understand your rights in a relationship and to separate fact from fiction. However, you can see that partners' beliefs about relationships can be very different, so it is important to start with one basic fact that supercedes all family and cultural teachings and to which both partners agree. Our underlying fact, the Starting Agreement, will form the foundation for this book.

Chapter Two

A STARTING AGREEMENT

Here Is One Fact Upon Which You Must Agree

The Baseline for Understanding and Communication

Even though you are in a relationship, you are still a human being, aren't you? You and your partner are not aliens from two different planets. You are two humans from Earth. You aren't joined at the hip and one person is not an extension of the other. You are unique individuals with more similarities than differences.

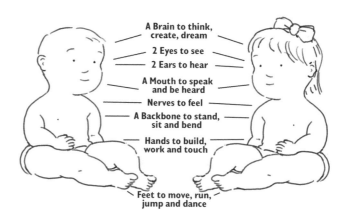

A Brain to think, create, dream

2 Eyes to see

2 Ears to hear

A Mouth to speak and be heard

Nerves to feel

A Backbone to stand, sit and bend

Hands to build, work and touch

Feet to move, run, jump and dance

Fact: in a relationship, you and your partner are both individual human beings.

Although men and women are biologically different, most of the differences in the ways partners treat each other are superficial. We learn how to treat each other from our families, cultures, and environments. These are expectations based on what we have learned from those around us. They are not based on the human qualities with which each of us is born. Many people have been taught that men and women have specific roles, regardless of personal abilities or interests. But not all women are alike and not all men are alike, so why should all roles and relationships be alike?

Being in a relationship does not mean that you and your partner are joined at the hip and share the same organs or brains. All human beings still have their own feelings, five senses, and human qualities. All human beings are created in the same way regardless of gender, race, or age. Each of us has the right to develop our human qualities and to be respected as individuals in a relationship. If your partner is unwilling to accept you as an individual human being, you might want to reconsider being in the relationship at all!

Entering into a relationship does not mean granting permission for your partner to direct or control you. Instead, a relationship should be a means of enhancing and enriching each partner as an individual in all areas of his or her life:

- as an individual
- as a partner
- as a parent (if there are children)

Each person needs to choose the right balance for his or her life, as an individual, a partner, and a parent. No one can decide the right balance for you. No one can tell you how you should feel.

- Just because one person earns more money doesn't mean that person should control the other. That's like buying a slave, and slavery was abolished with the Emancipation Proclamation of 1863.
- Just because one partner is a man and another is a woman doesn't mean that one person should control or be controlled by the other. That's sexist and bigoted.
- Just because one partner's parents had a lopsided relationship that somehow lasted for thirty, forty, or fifty-plus years doesn't mean that the behavior wasn't hurtful to one or both partners or that the next generation needs to continue it.

YOUR RELATIONSHIP RIGHTS ARE BASED ON AN IMPORTANT AGREEMENT

Both partners come into the relationship from different families and backgrounds, so what do you do if the partners' beliefs about relationships aren't the same? Whose expectations are right and whose are wrong? Both partners could truly love each other but not understand each other's expectations. Therefore, in order for both partners to be on the same Relationship Road with the same road map to *Happily-Ever-After*, they need to begin with a new relationship agreement that supercedes both of their backgrounds and that they both can accept.

When couples go into counseling, most start with criticism and complaining about their differences. The complaining may go on and on and on and the couples may drift further and further apart. *Relationship Rights (and wrongs)* is different. Instead of starting with differences, *Relationship Rights (and wrongs)* starts with an agreement that it is hard for either partner to refute. Then all behaviors in the relationship can be measured according to the starting agreement rather than prior expectations. There is a basis for agreement now between the two partners for communicating and understanding that supercedes earlier differences in expectations.

This new agreement is the basis for reevaluating and if necessary resetting each partner's expectations. Here, we establish each partner's Relationship Rights.

At this point, you are probably reading this book without your partner and planning to do your Relationship Reality Check alone. Later in the book, you will have the option to share this important Partners' Starting Agreement with your partner. But for now, affirming your belief in the Partners' Starting Agreement is a good beginning. You might also want to refer back to it at various times during your Relationship Reality Check to reevaluate how strongly you feel your partner supports or denies the agreement in your relationship.

The first step in your Relationship Reality Check is agreeing to the following statement. If you agree, repeat the Partners' Starting Agreement several times to reaffirm your understanding.

PARTNERS' STARTING AGREEMENT

Both partners in a relationship are individual human beings and deserve to be treated that way.

In addition to a starting agreement, we also need to make sure we are all using the same definitions of "love" and "relationship." This way we know that we are expecting to go to the same place, *Happily Ever After*, and that we can get there together. Without the same definitions, the same words may mean different things to each partner.

SOME MEANINGS OF THE WORD *LOVE*

Meaning 1)

One person idolizes another but expects nothing in return. Examples of this are as follows: girls over the years have said they *love* Frank Sinatra, Paul McCartney, Leonardo di Caprio, or Ricky Martin, and boys have *loved* Marilyn Monroe, Christie Brinkley, Halle Berry, or Britney Spears. However, the celebrities don't necessarily know the girls or boys who love them.

This is a one-sided love.

There is no measure of success.

Meaning 2)

Young girls often say they *love* dogs, horses, or their Barbie® dolls. Young boys might say they *love* dinosaurs, football, or bugs.

This is love but not of a human kind.

There is no human measure of success.

Meaning 3)

Parents say to their children "I *love* you," or sisters and brothers might say it to each other. This is a very deep affection and caring with absolutely no sexual overtones. It makes a child realize how much his or her parents care and makes him or her feel special and cherished.

This is a love of a familial kind.

Its success is measured by the warmth and self-concept built by communicating this love to a child or family member.

Meaning 4)

When some people say "I *love* you," it means, "I care about what you do for me but not about you as an individual." This can mean such things as, "You make me look good," "You're a good financial provider," "You support my needs," "You will make a good mother or father for my children," or anything else. This is similar to the old Toyota commercial jingle, "I love what you do for me!" This is an unemotional love. It need not be concerned about the feelings or needs of the other person. The partner could just as well be a car, a bus, or a train, if it fills the other partner's needs. You are the vehicle for fulfilling your partner's needs.

This is a needy "vehicle" love.

Its success is measured by how well one partner fulfills the other partner's needs. Both partners' needs do not have to be fulfilled or enhanced.

Meaning 5)

When some people say "I *love* you," it doesn't mean "I care about you as a separate person." Instead, it means the opposite, "I want to own you; I want to control you." This love is intense and therefore seems caring at the beginning. However, as the relationship develops, the controlling ownership nature takes over. In the early stages of this kind of relationship, it is difficult to discern the difference between the caring and the controlling.

This is a controlling, possessive love.

Its success is measured by how well one partner controls and the other accepts submission and servitude, not necessarily the happiness or development of both partners.

Meaning 6)

Some people want sex, companionship, financial support, or some other personal need fulfilled and they use the word "love" to get it. When they say, "I love you," they may mean, "Jump into bed with me," "I'm lonely," or, "I need financial help." The meaning of love is irrelevant.

This is a hollow love.

Its success is only related to how long the partners stay together to fulfill their different needs.

Meaning 7)

Sometimes in relationships two people come together from different backgrounds with different interests, or they may come together from similar backgrounds with similar interests, but in either case, these couples have one thing in common: they have partners who care, respect, support, and encourage each other as separate individuals, as well as sharing their lives and individuality together. They show their love by connecting with each other. They want their partners to become the best they can be as individuals because this will add more to their relationship. Their love for each other is non-judgmental and unconditional. This type of relationship, regardless of the partners' backgrounds, is a mutual and intimate giving, caring, and sharing between two people. Both partners respect each other's personal qualities, and each freely gives of himself or herself to support the other. They take joy in each other, which radiates its own energy back to the partners. It is like a continuous electrical circuit between the partners creating mutual power, energy, and excitement.

This is a mutually supportive love.

Its success is measured by the closeness, mutual happiness, and growth of both partners.

**FOR *RELATIONSHIP RIGHTS (AND WRONGS)*,
WE USE MEANING #7 FOR "*LOVE.*"**

SOME MEANINGS OF THE WORD *RELATIONSHIP*

Meaning 1)

Two people come together for convenience. The union does not have any intimacy or real sharing. Both partners usually receive some mutual benefit such as sharing the cost of living or other tasks and obligations. Otherwise, the partners are free to go on their merry ways without showing any concern for each other. This is a valid relationship, but both partners must understand that its basis is only convenience, and they should not expect much more.

This is a convenient relationship.

Its success is measured by how long the convenience lasts.

Meaning 2)

Two people come together in an intimate union in which one partner controls, the other submits. In this situation, one person is the ruler of the relationship. The terms and conditions of the union are entirely in the hands of the ruler. The submissive partner cannot dissent. The ruler need not show any concern for the individuality or the feelings of any submissive parties. In this type of relationship, the partners both must understand and accept these terms. For example, if the submissive partner isn't aware that his or her life is supposed to be totally controlled by the other, then one or both partners might be hurt. However, if both partners are willing to accept these terms, this, too, can be a valid, lasting relationship.

This is a ruling relationship.

Its success is measured by how well the ruler can enforce the obedience of the submissive partner (or other submissive family members).

Meaning 3)

Two people come together for a relationship and are inseparable. The two partners do everything together, go to each other for permission to do anything, have the same opinions, and cannot act alone. This appears to be a totally respectful and caring relationship, but in fact, neither partner is capable of acting as an individual. It is impossible to see where one partner stops and the next one begins. Their individuality is totally indistinguishable.

This is an enmeshed relationship.

Its success is measured by the loss of individuality of each of the partners.

Meaning 4)

Two people come together in an intimate union with respect, care, support, and sharing of each other's feelings, needs, interests, and growth as separate individuals. The partners can come from similar or different backgrounds and can have other similarities and differences between them, but they accept, respect, and love each other as they are. Both partners encourage each other to grow as individuals and also give back to the relationship. Both partners must give of themselves and share, but due to this mutuality, both experience enhancement, satisfaction, and individual growth.

This is a mutually supportive relationship

Its success is measured by the warmth, development, fulfillment, and happiness of both partners.

**FOR *RELATIONSHIP RIGHTS (AND WRONGS)*,
WE USE MEANING #4 FOR *"RELATIONSHIP."***

WE ALL WANT TO FEEL SUCCESSFUL, BUT WHAT DOES SUCCESS MEAN?

Finally, different cultures have different measures of success for husbands and wives in relationships. People grow up with these different relationship expectations, both good and bad, based on how they were brought up. One partner may have expected to be dominant while the other had to be totally submissive. These relationships may have worked, because both partners grew up with the same cultural expectations. They planned to live up to their respective roles, despite being repressive or hurtful, because these were the only roles they knew. Other couples may have grown up with mutually supportive partnership role models that encouraged the development and respect of both partners. Whatever the expectations, these are the roles to which couples measure their success as a partner.

How do you and your partner measure success for yourselves in your relationship? Is it with the same role expectations? Unfortunately, love is blind and people don't realize that their partner may have grown up with a different cultural expectation of a successful husband or wife until they marry or commit to the relationship. For example, the roles for successful husbands and wives in cultures A and B below show how different cultural expectations may be.

CULTURE A: Relationship Role Expectations

A successful husband is measured by:

- How much money you have in the bank
- How well you control your wife
- How obedient your children are

A successful wife is measured by:

- How obedient you are to your husband
- How much you do for your husband and family
- How much you give up of yourself

CULTURE B: Relationship Role Expectations

A successful husband is measured by:

- How much money you give to charity
- How well you treat your wife
- How happy and successful your children are

A successful wife is measured by:

- How much you help support your husband's success
- How you develop your potential
- How happy and successful your children are

If you were a woman and grew up in Culture A, married a man from Culture A, and then went to a counselor or a pastor for marriage counseling, you might be told, "Just go back and try a little harder." If you became more obedient and gave up more of yourself, your husband would be happy and everything might work out. Whereas, if you grew up in culture B and married someone from culture A, you might be in for a culture shock and not understand what was wrong. The more you tried to develop your own potential, the madder your husband might get. He might feel threatened while you thought you were making him proud and happy.

As individuals in relationships, we follow what we have learned. If we are not taught that there are alternative cultural expectations and role models available for relationships, we don't know anything different. We all deserve to see and learn about different relationship roles and expectations so that we can choose for ourselves.

A prevailing attitude in counseling is, "You must accept him (or her) for what he (or she) is." It is one thing to ask people to accept their partners' differences of opinion, tastes, interests, etc. This is respectful of the differences between individuals. However, it is another matter to ask people to accept their partners' bad, controlling, or hurtful behaviors toward them as "what he (or she) is." Telling people that they must accept all of their partners' behaviors as "what he (or she) is" absolves the counselor of responsibility of teaching alternative and more respectful behaviors. It assumes that people know alternative role models. It assumes that partners are choosing to be as they are based on full knowledge of alternative role models. The obvious reason many "regular" people go to marriage counseling is to learn alternatives in order to help solve their partnership differences. If partners knew all the alternative role models from which they could choose, they would likely not have so many problems.

Old stereotype roles may have served a purpose in other generations, but with more two-income families, cultural intermarriages, and advanced technology, we need to learn more about alternative cultural expectations.

For *Relationship Rights (and wrongs)*, there are no cultural expectations or stereotypes like those above. Each partner is treated as an individual.

RELATIONSHIP GOAL

Both partners in a relationship deserve to be enhanced as individuals as a result of being in the relationship.

Do both you and your partner agree to the Relationship Goal? Then your actions toward each other should match this goal. Do they?

SLOW DOWN FOR THIS EXTRA THOUGHT

I always believe we are the same; we are all human beings. Of course there may be differences in cultural background or way of life, there may be differences in our faith, or we may be of a different color, but we are human beings, consisting of the human body and the human mind. Our physical structure is the same, and our mind and our emotional nature are also the same. Wherever I meet people, I always have the feelings that I am encountering another human being, just like myself. I find it is much easier to communicate with others on that level. If we emphasize specific characteristics, like I am Tibetan or I am Buddhist, then there are differences. But those things are secondary. If we can leave the differences aside, I think we can easily communicate, exchange ideas, and share experiences.

His Holiness the Dalai Lama and Howard C. Cutler, M.D.

Chapter Three

HOW DO YOU KNOW WHERE YOU ARE?

Do You Have a Map to Happily-Ever-After?

When you are trying to get to a destination, but instead find yourself side-tracked or lost, you need to stop along the way to get your bearings or ask for directions. You want to get back on course, but you don't have a map.

You can't ask the people around you or passersby for directions, because they don't know where you are going or how to get there. So you call the place to which you are going, because they know the directions better than anyone else. You say, "We're lost. How do we get to your place?" Do they then say to you?...

- "Here are the skills you need to get here." *Skills help for survival, but they don't give you directions to your destination.*
- "Put together a list of where you went wrong and then you can figure out how to get back on course." *You don't know where you went wrong, because there wasn't a map in the first place.*

- "There are lots of 'how-to' books in the glove compartment." *A how-to book isn't good unless you know where to begin.*

Or are you first asked...
- "Where are you now?"

Before anyone can give you advice, you need to know and explain where you are in order to get directions to go somewhere else.

Unfortunately, in the relationship world, there wasn't a map or a list of benchmarks for us to use to understand or explain where we were in our relationship, on the way to *Happily-Ever-After*. We didn't know where we made wrong turns because there was no map, it was hard to make a list because we there were no standards or benchmarks, how-to books were one step beyond us, and teaching us skills wasn't going to help us find our way because we didn't recognize where we were in the first place.

The best means to get a map or a guide to a destination is to follow couples that are already there. They know the way.

We were looking for couples in healthy, mutually supportive relationships who could give us the guidelines to *Happily-Ever-After*, since they were already there. What were the elements in common among these couples to help them reach *Happily-Ever-After*?

In the relationship world we saw hundreds of "how-to" books, plenty of skill building programs, and thousands of experts who talked about relationships, but nowhere could we find a simple list of the elements found in most healthy, mutually supportive relationships.

We discovered that other people were just as confused as we were. They couldn't clearly identify where they were in their relationships. They often felt confused, hurt, afraid, stunted in their personal growth, numb, or ambivalent. When they tried to share these concerns with their partners, their partners would counter with such responses as:

"This is the way it's supposed to be."
"This is how my parents were, and look at how long they have been together."
"This is what all my friends do; what's the matter with you?"
"You're ungrateful."

In our relationships, we were confused by our partners' responses. We felt we were in unhealthy relationships, but we didn't know exactly where we were on the Relationship Road or how to move forward. Do we speak up, walk out, or keep going? For Beth, she and her husband pulled off to the side of the road and went to marriage counselors. They both wanted to make the marriage work. However, in this case the counselors made them feel as though they were crazy. Beth felt she was just unaccepting, petty, or not a good communicator. The counselors told her that she just had to learn how to live with the situation or try harder to communicate, as if the relationship were healthy as long as Beth learned to live with it. So they just kept going in the same direction for another five, then ten, and finally eighteen years. Beth's family and friends also tried to rescue her and whisk her out of the situation, but she wasn't sure whether she should go with them and take their advice. After all, the counselors were professional—they told her she just had to learn how to live with the situation and that she was imagining the problem. Therefore, how would any other relationship be different? This was Beth's relationship, not her parents', sisters', or friends' relationship. On the other hand, Melinda's family urged her to stay, even though the relationship was hurting her. They said, "That's just the way things are," or "Try a little harder." In both situations, we were confused and needed clear direction, but we had no map or benchmarks to share with our partners, counselors, parents, or friends. We knew we weren't in *Happily-Ever-After*, but where were we?

YOU NEED A CHECKLIST OF YOUR RELATIONSHIP RIGHTS.

If you don't recognize where you are, how can you get directions to go somewhere else?

If you don't know what you should have, how will you know when something is missing?

If you don't know what is right, how will you know when something is wrong?

In real life, auto insurance companies ask for the make, model, and serial number of your car so they have a record in case of loss. Credit card protection companies ask you to send a list of all your credit cards and their numbers so that if one is lost or stolen, they have a record. Insurance companies ask you to photograph furniture and other personal belongings in the house so they can see what is missing if there's a robbery or your home is destroyed.

But do you have a list of what you should have in a relationship, something you live with every day of your life? A list that would show you what is missing in your relationship? Cars are traded in every few years, credit cards are updated and replaced, but for something so important as a life-long relationship upon which you will build a future, were you ever taught or given a list of what to do or expect with your partner? Have you ever seen a list of the qualities found in healthy, mutually supportive relationships? If you want that kind of a relationship, wouldn't you like to have this list to share with your partner?

We have researched and gathered such a list of the qualities found in loving, mutually supportive relationships that we call your Relationship Guide. It is based on a mutually acceptable starting point—the Partners' Starting Agreement, which states that "Both partners in a relationship are individual human beings who deserve to be treated that way." It identifies for both men and women the common qualities we found in these relationships. This is your checklist to evaluate what you have in your relationship. Will you have all the essential qualities you need to move along the Relationship Road to *Happily-Ever-After*?

Let's look at how this list can help get your relationship to *Happily-Ever-After*.

Chapter Four

CHECK YOUR RIGHTS AT THE RELATIONSHIP TRAFFIC LIGHT

What Are Your Green, Yellow, and Red Relationship Rights?

Now that your Partners' Starting Agreement and key definitions are in place, you're ready to begin thinking about your Relationship Rights. But where do you begin? Relationships are complex. There are some behaviors you expect to find in a relationship and there are other behaviors you don't expect to see in a relationship, while there are also benefits you expect to gain. How do you sort this all out and keep it simple?

Think of traffic lights. They are built to clarify and direct traffic. But what happens if everyone has different meanings of Green, Yellow, and Red lights? Instead of all the drivers on the road instinctively communicating and understanding each other, there is chaos. Horns are beeping, tempers are flaring, accidents happen, and traffic comes to a halt. As you drive merrily down the Relationship Road with your partner toward *Happily-Ever-After*, what happens when you come to a traffic light? Do both of you have the same meanings of

Green, Yellow,, and Red? What happens to your relationship? How do you sort out what to do and where to go?

We all have internal traffic lights inside each of us that tell us "Go," "Caution," and "Stop" in life's situations. We recognize these feelings when they appear in our relationships, but we aren't sure our partners understand the same meanings of Green, Yellow, and Red. This causes confusion in our own minds and with our partners. We found that partners in healthy, mutually supportive relationships have the same meanings for Green, Yellow, and Red behaviors in their relationships. They instinctively communicate and support each other's rights like multiple cars at a traffic light.

We compiled the lists of "Go," "Caution," and "Stop" behaviors found in healthy, mutually supportive relationships into a one-page format we call your Relationship Guide. This gives both partners the same meanings for Green, Yellow, and Red behaviors in a relationship. We call these your Green, Yellow, and Red Rights. With a common guide in front of them, both partners will have the same meanings for Green, Yellow, and Red Rights to communicate and support each other.

Following is a brief overview of these rights. Before you can evaluate your relationship, you need to understand these three categories of Relationship Rights. Only then can you and your partner decide how you should proceed down the Relationship Road to *Happily-Ever-After.*

GREEN RIGHTS: GO WITH YOUR PERSONAL RESOURCES

PERSONAL RIGHTS

These are the personal resources with which you were born and that make you unique.

Green Rights represent the qualities that come from inside you and that make you a unique individual. You should take these rights with you wherever you go, whether you are in a relationship or single. They should never be denied you, taken away, or controlled by another person. These Green Rights need to be respected in order for you to develop your full potential as a human being and to identify you as a unique person.

Green Rights Questions

Mark "T" next to the statement in each pair that best fits your feelings about your relationship.

1a ___ Do you feel good about yourself as an individual and your capabilities and accomplishments when you are with your partner?

b ___ Do you feel better about yourself everywhere else (such as at work, at school, in the community, or with friends) than when you are with your partner?

2a ___ Do you feel you are able to develop your talents and interests?

b ___ Do you feel your partner is holding you back or controlling your development as an individual?

3a ___ Do you feel you have the right to make choices or decisions, and does your partner support you?

b ___ Do you feel your partner has to approve of all decisions you make, and if you make a decision, does your partner often criticize or sabotage it?

4a ___ Are you able to make your own choices about how you spend your time?

b ___ Do you feel your partner dictates how you should spend your time or makes you feel guilty for taking time for yourself?

5a ___ Does your relationship reflect your opinions, tastes, friends, and interests as well as your partner's?

b ___ Does your partner always have to get his or her way in the relationship or else you may suffer later in a different way?

Results

If you answered "T" to the first question in each pair, your partner supports your personal rights in your relationship.

If you answered "T" to the second question in each pair, you might have concerns about your personal rights and development as an individual. Your Green Rights are not being supported. They deserve respect because they are a part of you.

YELLOW RIGHTS: CAUTION IF YOU AREN'T GETTING ENOUGH BENEFITS

BENEFIT RIGHTS

These are the rights you gain from being in a relationship.

Both partners should receive relationship benefits. If there were no benefits in relationships, then everyone would be happier staying single or just living with a roommate. However, a person can gain distinct and wonderful benefits if he or she is willing to be part of a meaningful relationship. But neither partner should get all of his or her rights at the expense of the other; both partners need to yield so that there is mutual give and take.

Yellow Rights Questions

Mark "T" next to the statement in each pair that best fits your feelings about your relationship.

1a ___ Do you feel your relationship with your partner is special and still creates sparks and warmth?

 b ___ Do you feel your relationship with your partner has become so blah or unemotional that you could almost be living with a roommate?

2a ___ Do you feel your partner appreciates you as a person as well as what you do in the relationship?

 b ___ Do you feel taken for granted or unappreciated for who you are as an individual and what you do?

3a ___ Do you look forward to sharing experiences or going places with your partner because it makes the good times even better?

 b ___ Would you often rather do things alone, or with someone other than your partner?

4a ___ Does your partner support you through problems or troubled times and make them easier to handle?

 b ___ During problem or troubled times, would you rather handle things alone or even avoid sharing them with your partner?

5a ___ Is your relationship fun?

 b ___ Is your relationship a chore?

Results

If you answered "T" to the first question in each pair, you are receiving relationship benefits.

If you answered "T" to the second question in each pair, you may not be gaining many benefits from being in the relationship and might want to see what can be done to improve it. Your Yellow Rights need work to build up the benefits.

RED RIGHTS: STOP TOLERATING HURTFUL BEHAVIORS

YOUR SAFETY RIGHTS
Each partner has the right to be safe from harmful behaviors.

Hurt can be subtle and not necessarily physical. One partner's behaviors can harm the other psychologically and emotionally. These forms of hurt can be far more damaging than bruises. Bruises usually heal over time, but psychological damage lingers. The Red Rights represent safety from behaviors you should never have to tolerate from your partner. These behaviors are harmful and destructive and should be stopped immediately.

Red Rights Questions

Mark "T" next to the statement in each pair that best fits your feelings about your relationship.

1a   ___ Do you look forward to being with your partner?

 b   ___ Are you often afraid or dread being with your partner?

2a   ___ Do you usually feel free to be yourself in your relationship?

 b   ___ Do you often feel you have to be "on guard" or walk on eggshells for fear of setting your partner off?

3a   ___ Do you feel comfortable with the balance in your relationship?

 b   ___ Do you ever feel crazy not knowing how much you should tolerate in order to be considered a supportive partner?

4a   ___ Do you miss your partner when you are apart?

 b   ___ Do you feel relief when you are away from your partner?

5a __ Is your partner usually understanding and caring about your feelings?

b __ Have you built a wall around yourself to protect yourself from your partner's comments?

6a __ Is your home a positive environment with your partner?

b __ Is your relationship full of negativity, complaints, judgments, and criticism?

Results

If you answered "T" to the first question in each pair, you are safe in your relationship.

If you answered "T" to the second question in each pair, your partner is hurting you. Your Red Rights are being violated. You can stop tolerating hurtful behaviors as justification for supporting your partner. You deserve to feel safe when you are with your partner.

SLOW DOWN FOR THIS EXTRA THOUGHT

TREAT ME AS AN INDIVIDUAL

When I ask you to listen to me
And you start GIVING ADVICE,
you have not done what I asked.

When I ask you to listen to me
And you feel you have to SOLVE MY PROBLEM,
You have failed me, strange as that may seem.

When I ask you to listen to me
And you tell me why I SHOULDN'T FEEL THAT WAY,
You are trampling on my feelings.

LISTEN! All I asked was that you listen, not talk or do.

You must accept that I am a separate and individual
human being from you.
When you can accept as a simple fact that I feel what I
feel...
No matter how irrational or how strange my feelings
may seem to you,
Then you are able
   to listen,
   and understand,
   and accept me as my own person.

So, please, listen and just hear me.
And if you want to talk, wait a minute for your turn...
And I'll listen to you.

(adapted from an unknown author)

CERTIFICATE
OF
BIRTH

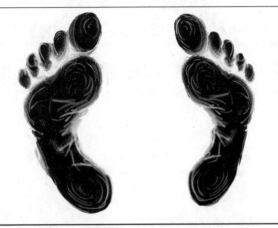

PERSONAL RESOURCES
INCLUDED

Feelings Achievements Talent
Creativity Opinions Energy
Dignity Friends Health Spirituality
Health Spirituality Dignity Friends
Achievements Energy Opinions

Green Rights are the personal rights that you were born with.
They are the DNA that makes you who you are.

They should always GO with you.

Chapter Five

YOUR PERSONAL RIGHTS: GREEN RIGHTS

GO with Your Personal Resources Everywhere Whether You're in a Relationship or Not

The first light on our relationship traffic light is green, which represents the rights you are born with. Green Rights are your personal rights and always belong to you. These rights stay with you whether you are in a relationship or single.

Your Green Rights are:

Achievements	Feelings	Reality
Balance	Financial Discretion	Safe Haven
Creativity & Ideas	Friends	Space
Dignity	Health	Spirituality
Dreams & Goals	Intelligence	Talents & Career
Energy	Motivations	Time
Family Ties	Opinions & Tastes	

These Green Rights are internal belongings that come from inside your heart, mind, and body. They distinguish you as an individual and should be part of you wherever you are. Just as no two people have the same DNA, no two people have the same mix of personal qualities.

What does this mean to the dream of our Charming Prince and Fair Princess?

Most of us picture the Charming Prince and Fair Princess supportive of each other. Since they fell in love with each other as unique individuals with that passionate sparkle in their eyes, we believe they will continue to love each other as unique individuals. They loved the distinctive qualities that made them who they are—their Green Rights. They sought each other out as individuals, they love each other as individuals, and they will grow as individuals, further sharing themselves and building an even stronger relationship.

So when the Prince and Fair Princess ride off together toward *Happily-Ever-After*, in your wildest imagination would you ever picture one saying to the other, "Now that we are riding off on the Relationship Road together, I don't love you for who you really are; I'm going to change you into someone else?" And just like that, "POOF," the Prince changes the Fair Princess into a frog that will hop along with him and fit in his hip pocket to be removed whenever he needs something from her. Or maybe it is the Fair Princess who changes the Prince into a frog. Either way, being the frog wouldn't be fun, especially if you were never warned of this before you entered the relationship.

Frogs don't do much except hop along, croak, eat bugs, and fit into a shoebox or someone's pocket. They don't have the human qualities that allow them to think, dream, create, build, have feelings, and do other things that humans do. When a partner asks us to give up our human qualities in order to be controlled, we become creatures like frogs without the ability to use or control our lives and ourselves.

However, in the real world where partners can respect each other's Green Rights, the Charming Prince and Fair Princess can love and respect each other for who they are. They do not try to change each other into frogs or anything else. All their human qualities are respected and honored in the relationship. They accept and treat each other as unique individuals.

In a mutually supportive relationship where both individuals are respected, no one has the right to deny, change, control, or dictate your personal qualities.

- Your partner shouldn't try to **deny or change** your personal rights to make them the same as his or hers—that would make you just a copy.
- Your partner shouldn't want to **control** your personal rights—that would make you a slave, a possession, a trophy, a toy, or a frog.
- Your partner shouldn't want to **dictate** your personal rights—that would prevent you from reaching your full potential and leave you less than a whole person.

WHEN YOU HAVE YOUR GREEN RIGHTS, YOU FEEL FREE TO DEVELOP

When your partner respects your Green Rights, you don't feel that anyone other than yourself is dictating your choices. You can be uninhibited, motivated, and goal oriented. If you choose to pursue them, your goals appear attainable. You don't need to go back to someone else to get permission for decisions about yourself. You don't feel held back or weighed down by your partner's interference in your personal decisions. There is mutual understanding, support, encouragement, and even excitement between you and your partner.

HOW CAN YOU LOSE SOMETHING THAT IS INSIDE OF YOU?

The truth is that sometimes you don't realize what you are losing while it is happening. Unfortunately, until you get into a relationship, you don't always know what is in your partner's head or what your partner's expectations for you are. When people start courting, they treat each other like royalty. They are on their best behavior. You think this relationship will be wonderful. It looks like the Charming Prince and Fair Princess are heading off to *Happily-Ever-After*. But at some point your partner's behaviors might change, and the relationship might become different than what you expected. You might react and try to fix things and think that you did something wrong. Then, your Relationship Rights start to change. They usually disappear a little at a time so that you hardly notice while you are trying to make things better. At first, you feel a little strange but can't identify the exact problem. Finally, so many of your personal qualities disappear that you might not even recognize yourself or the personal rights that define you. Yet you still believe that your partner loves you as much as before and that you are still heading toward *Happily-Ever-After* together. You can't believe that your partner would take your rights and hurt you. After all, isn't this the individual who professes to love and care about you?

You can lose your personal rights in one of two ways—either with or without knowledge.

Some people freely give up their rights to their partner because from the time they are born, they are taught that their role in a relationship is to be submissive and let their partner control them. In this case, you're a submissive partner who feels responsible for keeping the relationship together and expects to lose your personal rights. You probably don't know anything different. You believe that your partner cares about you, so you will not be hurt. This makes it safe and okay to be submissive. With this group, the fallacy comes when your partner doesn't care about your personal qualities, personal needs, or if you are developmentally, emotionally, and sometimes physically hurt. You never expect to reach your potential as an individual because your goal is to be with a partner who controls you. You put your future in your partner's hands.

Other people might lose their personal rights because they don't recognize the process while it is happening. You believe your partner loves you for who you are and therefore would never want to control you, hurt you, or deny your rights. But that belief can be wrong. Your family background or culture may have different relationship ideals and measurements of success than your partner's, creating different expectations, although you are both in love. Also, your definitions of "love" and "relationship" are likely different from your partner's, but you don't realize it. Your partner might not love you as an individual who needs and deserves support for your personal rights, but rather you are loved for your value as a partner, more like a "needy vehicle" love. Your partner looks at you as being in the relationship solely to play a role and support your partner's needs. In this situation, your rights are gradually eroded and relinquished. You slowly give up your rights in the process of trying to please your partner, without realizing it is happening.

A CHECKLIST OF YOUR RELATIONSHIP RIGHTS

Before you got into a permanent relationship, did you make a checklist of your Relationship Rights? Did you list the personal rights (Green Rights) that always belong to you? Did you list the relationship benefits (Yellow Rights) that you should receive from the relationship? Did you list the harmful behaviors you should be safe from and not be asked to tolerate (Red Rights) in a relationship? Or, like most of us, did you just expect you were going to *Happily-Ever-After* but didn't have a list of what it might take to get there? Without this list of what to expect in a relationship, you might not know whether something is missing or not working.

Because people are not aware of their personal rights, they're not conscious when they are missing. People don't always recognize when they lose their personal rights; however, they might start feeling a little off balance, unsure of themselves, or confused.

People don't lose their rights all at once. They lose them a little at a time... a little here and a little there. They give in once, they give in twice, until a pattern forms. Then the rest go like dominoes. All their rights might be gone before they realize it.

Some people might lose only a few personal rights and can easily live without them. Others could lose most of their personal rights. It all depends on their partners' needs, their partners' insecurities, their partners' demands, and the importance of each right to a partner.

THREE WAYS ONE PARTNER CAN CONTROL ANOTHER'S GREEN RIGHTS

- *Assert Subtle Control*

    Your partner encourages you to do certain things and gets angry when you do others. Without direct orders, you learn what you can and can't do without making your partner angry. Your partner might allow you to clean the house but could get angry when you talk to friends on the phone. So as long as you're not on the phone and are working on the house, your partner is happy.

- *Assert Direct Control*

    Your partner gives you direct orders about what you can and can't do. When you disobey these orders, your partner criticizes you, punishes you, or becomes completely impossible to live with until you obey. Your partner might tell you when and how to do something or might tell you that you can't do something. If you don't follow the orders, you will pay for your disobedience in one way or another. You obey because it's easier to give up a personal right than pay the price for disobedience.

- *Assert Control through the Guise of Mutuality*

    Your partner believes that partners should get permission from each other to do things. When your partner asks permission for something, you always agree to the request because you want to support him or her (as you would in a mutually supportive relationship). However, when you ask your partner for something, your partner exercises veto power and regularly says no. The result is that your partner's rights are supported and yours are not. (This obviously is not a mutually supportive relationship, but you don't realize it.) You might support your partner's interests, talents, friends, or family, but your partner is not equally supportive of yours. Your partner never had any plans to support your requests, but through "the guise of mutuality," this procedure appears legitimate. This control is the most insidious and the hardest to identify.

REAL MUTUALITY IS ESSENTIAL FOR SUPPORTING EACH PARTNER'S GREEN RIGHTS

Certainly in a relationship a person deserves his or her Green Rights, but not at the expense of the other partner's Green Rights. Mutuality and compromise are necessary in any relationship. Each partner must willingly support the other's Green Rights. Some partners give of themselves only begrudgingly, and this type of support doesn't count. To have meaning, support must be positive and freely given.

You might have to exert great effort in convincing your partner to go to dinner with some of your friends. If your partner says, "I'll go, but I'm not going to like it," or as you are leaving says, "Let's not make it a late night," your partner starts the dinner with a chip on his or her shoulder. Actions such as these don't show true mutuality because support is not freely given and takes too much effort.

Or your partner might support you, but only once over a long period of time. Then when you ask for something, your partner says, "No, I've done that before." Or if you state that your partner doesn't support you, he or she replies, "I did support you. Remember that time two years ago?" Once or twice doesn't count. Mutual support must be regular, predictable, positive, and available without begging.

One partner should not demand rights all the time while not equally supporting the other partner's rights. It is both partners' responsibility to support each other's rights.

When you are close to a situation in which love is involved, you might have a hard time seeing what is actually happening in a relationship. You need to step back and do a Relationship Reality Check (Chapter Nine) of your Green Rights to see the whole picture of your personal rights.

SOME EXAMPLES OF GREEN RIGHTS IN RELATIONSHIPS

Nadine & Howard
When both partners support each other's Green Rights, both partners thrive.

Reality Bite...
Nadine grew up in an abusive home where she saw her father drink, often abuse her mother, and act emotionally absent from the family. Her mother was a caring and giving person and just tolerated Nadine's father's behavior because she felt she had to keep the relationship together. Her mother was a gifted pianist, but that all went away after she was married. To make sure she never played again, Nadine's father refused to buy a piano for their home. Nadine knew no other home and thought that this was the way married relationships were supposed to be.

When Nadine met Howard, he was from a different religion and culture. They fell in love despite their differences and married before she finished college. Nadine became the same kind of caring and giving partner as her mother. She worked to support Howard while he went through law school. She quit work to raise their two children and still supported Howard's interests, friends, and professional needs. Nadine expected little from Howard because that was the role model she saw while growing up. However, Howard came home each night (sober) to help with the kids. He encouraged Nadine to continue her schooling and develop outside interests in sports and other activities for herself. When she wanted to go on special out-of-town retreats, she didn't have to beg Howard for permission to go; he not only supported her going but also came home early to take care of the kids while she was gone. This was the culture in which Howard had grown up, where husbands want to make their wives feel special. Nadine and Howard's home was always safe, predictable, and free from angry outbursts or drinking binges. Both were growing as individuals and their children were thriving in the environment.

The reality is...

Nadine kept pinching herself to make sure this relationship was real and not imagined. She asked herself what she had done to deserve to be treated so well because her home was not the one she had seen as a child. She hadn't realized that all people deserve to have their Green Rights respected. Their kids are now grown and Howard and Nadine are empty-nesters with full lives of their own, as well as together. Nadine took up golf and goes out with Howard, and Howard learned how to play bridge so that he and Nadine could play together with friends. They have time to take walks and trips together but still have separate interests too. Both of their kids are married and have great relationships themselves because they had a great model, and now Nadine and Howard have six wonderful grandchildren to carry on the tradition.

Fran & Mark
When partners lose their Green Rights, they often don't realize what is happening until the rights are gone.

Reality Bite...

Fran finally left Mark, her husband of thirty years, at the age of fifty-two. Her leaving was prompted by the realization that one by one, she had given up the things that pleased her and made her different and independent. But at the time, she didn't realize what was happening. When they fell in love thirty years earlier, Mark couldn't spend enough time with Fran. His love seemed intense and enduring. She had never felt anyone be so in love with her before. She was sure this was the man who would adore her forever, so she married him.

Over the years, she continued to be supportive of Mark, their home, their children, and all of his interests, activities, friends, and family. Mark still wanted to control Fran's time when she was with him and even when she wasn't. But her husband started finding reasons for not visiting her family, yet always insisted on her entertaining his. He no longer wanted to go out with her friends and their husbands, so one by one she was cut off from them. She gave up her job. Her outside interests such as riding, swimming, and volunteering at the hospital also tapered off and ended. Mark took over all the household finances. Fran had no idea how much money her husband made or their financial condition. She was expected to buy groceries and pay the household expenses out of a budget that was too small to cover them, so she had to dip into the little savings she had put away while she was working. Every two years he wanted a new car, and while she was working, she had to provide most of the money for that, too. The car that he bought for Fran was now fifteen years old and badly in need of repair. It was unsafe for her to drive, but he didn't seem to worry as long as he still had his new car. Over the years, when she tried to discuss any of her concerns or feelings with him, he would get angry and call her an ungrateful partner. That made her feel confused, so she tried even harder to please him and thought he was right. (Otherwise why would he make such hurtful statements when he said he loved her?) It was less painful to endure the loss of her friends, family, and interests than to handle the anger, name-calling, and threats. So, she endured the loss of her personal rights in silence and increasing isolation. But the more she gave, the more he managed to find wrong.

Fran had believed "Do unto others as you would have them do unto you." That is the way mutually respectful relationships work. However, when one partner is not mutually respectful, the more you do for that person, the more that person takes. It is like giving yourself to a black hole or a bottomless pit. That partner doesn't "do back unto you" as the Golden Rule states. Finally, Fran was "all given out."

The reality is...

Fran was never hit or physically abused, but the loss of her personal qualities and rights killed her human spirit. It took away her human identity. She had given away everything. Yet, at the time, she never realized she was losing these personal rights; she just thought she was pleasing Mark and that at some time he in turn would please her. She still believed that he loved her and cared about how she felt. Finally, one morning she woke up and realized that she didn't recognize herself anymore. She knew she had to leave her marriage. Her husband had to approve her friends, family, and interests. She no longer had the ability to make decisions. She had to escape and become a whole person again. And so, after thirty years of marriage, she was alone again—but it was better than being a person she didn't recognize for another ten, twenty or thirty years.

Another look...

If Fran and Mark had known and respected each other's Green Rights:

Fran would have continued respecting, loving, and supporting her husband. However, her husband would also have respected, loved, and supported her. They would be going out together with not just his friends but hers as well. They would have time to spend with her family and his. She would still be able to have and develop outside interests such as riding, swimming, and volunteering at the hospital. Maybe her husband wouldn't get a new car every two years, but every four or five years instead, so that Fran could drive a newer, safer car, too. Fran would have been more informed about their financial position. She would have received a budget sufficient for the expenses she was required to pay, even if Mark had to cut back a little on his discretionary spending. And finally, Fran would not have been called names, be accused of being "ungrateful" or "a bad partner," or have to put up with Mark's anger. Mark would have respected her and discussed and resolved her concerns. Together, they would have recognized and respected each other as individuals.

Harriet & Harry
Green Rights involve give-and-take. No partner can get Green Rights at the expense of the other partner.

Reality Bite...

Harriet and Harry seemed like the perfect loving couple. He adored her and she adored him. They were together almost all of the time. Harriet supported Harry at his office by doing all of his clerical work and bookkeeping. At home they shared responsibilities. Harriet took care of the inside of the house, and Harry took care of the outside. Harriet would pick out the flowers and shrubs and Harry would plant and maintain them. Their yard was always meticulous and their grass was the greenest on the block. Harriet liked collecting 1950s and 60s memorabilia. So when Harry was finished with the yard, he would accompany Harriet to all the garage and rummage sales in the area so he could help her carry back all her purchases. Sometimes he would drive with her one-hundred miles just to get a particular collectible. But Harry also had a passion—the Green Bay Packers. On a game day, nothing would budge Harry out of his armchair in front of the television. Harriet resented this. She claimed she could take off all her clothes and jump up and down in front of him, but nothing would ever move him while the Packers were on. She said he loved the Green Bay Packers more than anything else, and this bothered her. She wanted Harry's attention all the time.

The reality is...

After the beginning of the NFL season, Harry and Harriet started arguing about the Packers. Harriet accused Harry of not loving her enough, or at least not as much as the Packers. At game time she wanted Harry to go with her to all her garage sales. Harry offered to go with her before or after the game, but that wasn't enough for Harriet. She wanted him all the time. Harriet called him selfish and uncaring. Harry was confused. He knew he did care a lot about the Packers, but did this mean he was selfish or that he had to give up the little bit of time he did ask for himself in order to be an unselfish and caring partner? Harry finally left the house for all Packer games and went to a sports bar to watch with his friends so he would not have to put up with Harriet's complaints and harassment. By the time Harry got home from the sports bar, he no longer wanted to go with Harriet to any garage sales. She was on her own!

After the Packers won the Super Bowl, Harriet was complaining about Harry to one of her divorced friends. Instead of being sympathetic, her friend told Harriet how selfish she was to expect to control all of Harry's time. She pointed out how supportive he was in all of Harriet's interests (including her rummaging) and told her that if she ever decided to leave Harry, she would gladly take him. Harriet was finally told off by her friend, and she finally realized that she was the one who was selfish, uncaring, and unsupportive. Harriet wouldn't accept the truth from Harry, but she would accept it from a friend. Why wouldn't she listen to her partner? (It would be so easy if partners would just listen to each other!)

Another look...

If Harry and Harriet had give and take of each other's Green Rights:

Harriet would have realized that she had no right to expect Harry to give up ALL of his interests in order to support hers. They both had a right to have their interests and have each other's support.

Harriet actually listened to Harry and accepted his interests as different from hers. She then understood that Harry wouldn't be able to go with her to every garage sale, but she appreciated when he did. Harry had a right to have his interests supported, too. And so, Harriet made sure that there was plenty of beer, potato chips, and Harry's favorite dip in the refrigerator for game time while she was gone on her rummaging. Both partners were happy and still did things together when they were finished with their interests.

SUMMARY CHARACTERISTICS OF GREEN RIGHTS

Green Rights are your Personal Rights that identify who you are as a person:

- *They identify your goals and achievements in life.*
- *They identify your family and friends with whom you surround yourself.*
- *They identify your interests and balance of these interests.*
- *They identify your mind, your opinions, what you think, and what you see.*
- *They identify your use of energy, money, time, and space.*
- *They identify your health, spirituality, and innermost feelings.*
- *Most of all, they identify your dignity and imprint as an individual human being.*

Below are definitions of your Green rights, and a brief description of how you may feel when they are supported or denied by your partner. If you want an expanded description of any of your Green Rights, a listing of the different aspects of each right in a relationship, or a more detailed explanation of how you may feel when they are supported or denied, go to www.relationshiprights.com.

YOUR ACHIEVEMENTS RESOURCE

Everybody completes tasks, jobs, projects, and goals. Each of these is an achievement. Some achievements are bigger, like winning an award, while some are smaller, like cleaning out a closet. Some achievements are more difficult, some are mundane, and some are exceptional. But still, everybody achieves things regularly and deserves to feel good about those achievements, no matter how big or small. When you know that your achievements count, you feel worthwhile as a person. Your achievements are an essential part of your self-esteem and self-confidence; all human beings have the right to choose and feel good about what they do.

- **Supported:** Your achievements let you feel that you are accomplishing things in your day and in your life.
- **Denied:** You may feel taken for granted or like a loser who can't accomplish things.

YOUR BALANCE RESOURCE

Everybody must find their own balance in life regarding their time, needs, and activities. Each person's balance of needs is different whether they are social, emotional, parental, physical, intellectual, creative, community, professional, spiritual, family, or other. Every individual knows what is needed for personal fulfillment in each area of his or her life. This balance of needs comes from inside each person. No one else can dictate what an individual's needs should be or what kind of balance should bring a partner happiness or fulfillment. At any point in time, your balance points may change as your life requirements change. Your partner must honor and respect your personal balance of needs because this balance is what makes you special and defines you as an individual.

- **Supported:** You feel peace of mind and body for that point in your life.
- **Denied:** Your life may feel off balance and unsatisfied, despite your best efforts.

YOUR CREATIVITY (AND IDEAS) RESOURCE

Everybody has the ability to make things, do new things, problem-solve, and have new thoughts. This ability comes from within. These are ways people express themselves and grow as individuals. They are intellectual and emotional outlets for people as well. The ability to create, make, do, and think helps us define what we like and who we are as individuals.

To have personal creativity and ideas, people need room to express themselves. Partners need to give each other time and space to develop their creativity, regardless of the other's talents in that area. Certainly you can't use your creativity and disregard your partner's feelings, but that doesn't mean your partner can control your time, resources, and means of expression. Your creative needs might be met by making a craft, doing a project, taking a class, playing a musical instrument, attending a program or lecture, working on a car, cooking, carpentry, or any other creative things you might like to do.

Personal creativity means that both partners have the right to express themselves in their own way in their relationship and in their home.

- **Supported:** Your mind and creative juices are stimulated and continue to flow.
- **Denied:** Your mind may feel stagnant or wasted.

YOUR DIGNITY RESOURCE

Everyone is special and every life is important. Therefore, everyone deserves to have a partner respect and accept his or her identity as a unique and worthy individual. You deserve to be treated by your partner with honor and esteem as an individual human being who has unique needs, interests, and wants. Dignity gives you the ability to maintain your own self-concept and self-worth, as well as being a partner to someone else. You should not have to lose your own identity because you are in a relationship. And, importantly, both partners must understand that each is worthy of a separate identity, apart from being the other's partner. When each partner has his or her dignity, each can give more to the relationship as individuals.

Dignity gives every human being the base and foundation for responding positively to life's challenges.

- **Supported:** You feel good about yourself as a person.
- **Denied:** You may feel that you are of little worth and it may be hard to motivate yourself.

YOUR DREAMS AND GOALS RESOURCE

Everybody has dreams and goals. These are dreams and goals about what you want to be or achieve in life. When you close your eyes and dream, how do you see yourself? These dreams and goals belong to you. Whether or not you can achieve these dreams, nobody has the right to crush them. These dreams give you hope and direction in life. This direction allows you to develop strategies to accomplish your goals. Without dreams and goals, you lack ambition and reasons for your actions.

Ideally, as a couple, partners share major goals and dreams together. However, partners should also have individual goals and dreams. Whatever your goals, as a couple or as an individual, they set directions and give your life purpose.

Every human being must be able to dream and have goals for the future. Without this vital resource, a person can become like a lost ship aimlessly floating at sea with no direction and no hope of ever reaching a final destination.

- **Supported:** You have direction in life and hope for the future.
- **Denied:** You may feel a lack of purpose in your actions and life.

YOUR ENERGY RESOURCE

Everybody creates energy to do things and makes decisions as to where to spend that energy. Each human being should be able to decide which activities deserve energy. For example, on a weekend, energy might go into work-related activities, children's activities, errands, cleaning, yard work, shopping, community service, a baseball game, fishing, or personal relaxation. Prioritizing personal energy and deciding what activities to complete first, second, third, and so on should be each individual's decision. Nobody has a right to dictate how another person's personal energy should be used.

Energy keeps us going like the battery in a car; it is a personal resource that needs to be used wisely so that it will be there whenever we need it.

- **Supported:** You are able to accomplish your goals and have balance in your life.
- **Denied:** You may feel drained with no energy to take care of yourself.

SLOW DOWN FOR THIS EXTRA THOUGHT

OUR EMOTIONAL ENERGY/OUR OWN ALWAYS-READY BATTERY

A person's emotional energy is like a battery. It needs to be constantly recharged so that we have enough energy for our daily life or in the case of a real emergency. A positive and mutually supportive relationship can keep recharging our energy for life or even make us super-charged. Optimism, freedom, creativity, solutions, and joy all create energy and help recharge a person's emotional batteries and can keep us running longer and stronger.

Just as a positive partner can supercharge us, a negative partner can drain us. A negative partner can regularly drain our energy by forcing us to respond to constant negative thoughts, judgments, criticism, and complaints. When this happens, we may have a hard time maintaining enough energy to get ourselves through the day. Responding to constant complaints, criticism, questioning, moaning about aches and pains, or listening to whining and nagging drains daily energy out of a person. Then, when real emergencies or problems arise that require our attention, our energy batteries are out of power. We have nothing left, because we have been drained for so long for no reason.

Do you want to be with an energy-drainer or an energy-maker?

YOUR FAMILY RESOURCE

Everybody deserves to have meaningful relationships with parents, grandparents, aunts, uncles, and cousins, and that doesn't mean just in name only. Family adds a sense of history, place, extended love, support, and comfort. When two people enter into a relationship, they leave their original families, but neither person should be forced to abandon their families or totally cut themselves off from family contacts. Certainly neither partner's family should interfere in a couple's establishment of family values or attempt to control the couple's time or decision-making. However, maintaining regular family contact and a sense of family roots are important for the continuity and richness of a relationship. Denying the personal resource of family does not make a person belong more to one's partner; it only cuts off roots and creates a lifetime of unresolved issues. Family is a resource that should not be taken for granted or ignored; it defines each human being's place in this world and gives us all a connection to our past, present, and future.

- **Supported:** You have a solid foundation, roots, and support and can build on your family outreach.
- **Denied:** You may feel disconnected and without closure in your life's passages.

YOUR FEELINGS RESOURCE

Everyone has a right to feelings. Feelings are never right or wrong; they just exist. No one can pass judgment on another person's feelings because feelings come from within the individual. Even though your feelings might be different from your partner's, they are still right for you. Feelings reflect each individual and his or her life experiences. No one can dictate or judge someone's being happy, sad, angry, glad, frustrated, anxious, excited, or nervous because everyone has had different life experiences. Through feelings, we understand and stay in touch with our inner selves.

Since both partners have feelings, whose feelings take priority? Your partner's feelings are not more important than yours. If your partner feels tired and doesn't want to go out and you feel cooped up, bored, and need to kick your heels, whose feelings are more important? There needs to be respect for both partner's feelings. Each situation is different and needs to reviewed and understood together.

However, partners must differentiate between having feelings and showing feelings. Although partners have the right to have feelings, they must be responsible for controlling how they show those feelings. Your partner doesn't have a right to hurt you by the way he or she shows feelings.

- **Supported:** You have a solid connection between what occurs on the outside and what you feel on the inside.
- **Denied:** You may feel out of touch or numb to what you see or what is done.

SLOW DOWN FOR THIS EXTRA THOUGHT

AN OLD ADAGE WITH AN ADDITION

(for those who don't know how to take responsibility for how they show their feelings):

*"If you don't have something nice to say...
don't say it at all*

UNLESS

*it will serve a useful purpose and
is done in a positive way."*

YOUR FINANCIAL DISCRETION RESOURCE

Everybody has a right to make individual financial decisions with some discretionary funds. This means that all partners need to have a way to get money in a non-demeaning manner, and they need to have a way to make purchases without being constantly judged. All of the relationship's discretionary money should not be kept in one person's control or so disproportionately divided that only one partner's needs are met while the other has to scrimp in order to meet a budget. A relationship needs flexibility and respect on both sides for making financial decisions. This is true whether both partners are working or one is working and the other is taking care of the home (which is a form of work). Mutuality should be present in the partners' spending and saving patterns. People deserve to have some financial parameters and flexibility in which they can make spending decisions without begging or being judged. Denying a partner financial parameters makes that person a slave and keeps him or her in relationship bondage and beholden to a keeper or the holder of the purse strings.

On the other side, overspending is also not acceptable. Overspending beyond the couple's means might unfairly force the responsible partner into over-extended financial obligations, insurmountable debt, or bad credit ratings. Financial parameters give a person dignity—both for spending and protection from over-spending.

- **Supported:** You have the financial respect of your partner and can maintain your dignity without groveling, because financial independence is power.
- **Denied:** You may feel like a servant or beholden to your partner.

YOUR FRIENDS RESOURCE

Everyone deserves to have his or her own friends. Friends are a necessary part of enrichment and support to any person's life. For each partner, they can supply an important outlet for sharing ideas, interests, activities, and thoughts. They can add to your life. To deny a person friends is to deny a person the right to a fulfilling life. It also places an almost unachievable burden on the partner to be everything to the other person.

Not all friends might be close to both partners, but that doesn't mean that you have to drop your friends because of your partner. Some friends are mutual to both partners, and some are one-sided, but in a relationship, both partners should show support for each other's friends. No one should be cut off from friends and their outside contacts.

Both partners deserve to have discretionary time with their friends. One partner does not own the other's time. This does not mean that "friends' time" should overrun the relationship, but it means that each partner deserves to be able to pick his or her friends and to be able to have some time with them without being judged or criticized.

- **Supported:** You can fulfill your interests and share ideas not held in common with your partner. This in turn relieves the burden on your partner for fulfilling all your needs or for being everything to you.
- **Denied:** You may feel isolated, without any sounding boards or outreach.

YOUR HEALTH RESOURCE

People are born with different bodies. Even among the sexes, some people have longer legs, others have faster metabolisms, and many have higher IQ's. Some people are born with disadvantages and disabilities. Whatever circumstances an individual is born with, he or she deserves the right to the time and ability to preserve his or her health and body through diet, exercise, and emotional outlets of his or her own choice.

- **Supported:** You are able to maintain physical and mental health for yourself and your family.
- **Denied:** You may lose your health and fitness or live with undue stress.

YOUR INTELLIGENCE RESOURCE

Everybody is born with a brain and the right to develop and use it. Personal intelligence gives individuals the ability to use their brains to make decisions and judgments, formulate beliefs and opinions, take actions, and listen to inner instincts. We are all smart enough to make personal decisions and to hold opinions without needing our partner's brainpower, approval, or permission. When we enter a relationship, we agree to work mutually as a couple, but that doesn't mean our partner has to approve every decision and opinion. We all deserve parameters in which to make decisions for the partnership, our families, or our children without requiring our partner's constant permission or judgment.

- **Supported:** You are able to function as a thinking human being capable of making decisions for yourself, the relationship, and your family.
- **Denied:** You may feel powerless or without control over your own life, since all decisions are made for you or require another's approval.

YOUR MOTIVATIONS RESOURCE

Everybody has reasons for doing things and acting certain ways. Personal motivations belong to each individual in a relationship and no one, not even a partner, can assign them to you because these motivations come from the inner self. Personal motivations are the basis for individual actions and statements. No one else can know another human being's personal motivations.

Human beings can be motivated to act out of joy, fear, necessity, pain, caring, concern, love, or whatever other reasons might exist. An action or statement might be motivated by a desire to please a partner or it might be self-pleasing. Sometimes motivations arise out of responsibility, such as child rearing or paying the rent. Whatever the motivation, it belongs to the individual. Instead of accepting your actions as legitimate, your partner might say to you:

"You only did that to make me mad."

"You're doing that to turn the kids against me."

"You didn't need to do that!"

- **Supported:** You and your actions are grounded in your own understanding and are respected by your partner.
- **Denied:** You might question your intentions. Your partner may be critical of your motivations.

YOUR OPINIONS AND TASTES RESOURCE

Everybody has opinions and tastes. An individual's opinions and tastes are just that, individual. They are always right for the individual and they can never be wrong. Nobody's opinions are stupid, and nobody's taste is bad.

What is important is that each partner's opinions and tastes are taken into consideration in a relationship. Both partners need to compromise. One partner cannot dictate all the couple's opinions and tastes, whether they are about spending/saving, friends, decorating, or recreational activities. Both partners deserve to feel validated and fulfilled and that their opinions and tastes are a part of the relationship. The relationship should be a blending and acceptance of the two partners.

- **Supported:** You can express yourself and maintain a sense of your own identity.
- **Denied:** You might feel that you are not a part of the relationship or are unworthy of expressing yourself.

YOUR REALITY RESOURCE

Everybody knows what is real. People know what really happens and what doesn't. They know what they see, hear, and do. Everyone, except perhaps people with mental illness, has the ability to differentiate between fact and fiction. Personal reality is an individual's knowledge of what actually happened. No matter what your partner might say or do in order to try to convince you, your reality belongs solely to you. Your reality is not created by your imagination or a sudden loss of memory but by things you know or remember.

This might sound strange, but often in relationships one partner tries to dictate another person's reality. Your partner might try to change the retelling of events that happened in order to fit his or her needs. This is called "rewriting history" and is described in the Red Rights. One partner might argue and get angry until the other partner agrees with the new version of the reality. Reality then becomes a big unknown instead of something real. Some common examples of a partner's distorting reality or rewriting history are:

"You never told me that!" (You know that you told your partner and even remember where and when you said it.)

"You never gave that to me." (You remember putting it in your partner's hands and seeing your partner carry it away.)

"I didn't put that there. You must have moved it." (You know that you never touched the object. And unless it flew through thin air, your partner must have put it there.)

"I never did that; you can't remember anything." (You saw your partner do "that" with your own eyes.)

"I never hit her. It was just a pat." (You saw the red marks on your child's body, and they couldn't have come from just a pat.)

- **Supported:** You have confidence in your reality and perceptions.
- **Denied:** You may feel you have lost your memory or your mind.

YOUR SAFE HAVEN RESOURCE

Everybody deserves a home that is safe. A home should be a "safe harbor from the storms of outside life." It should be a safe place to be and a safe place to be yourself. Everyone has a right to live in a place of peace. A home is a sanctuary where you are free to be yourself without fear of judgment.

A home should be a place of protection, a place of repose, a place to heal from the stresses and conflicts of the outside world. It should be free of risk, fear, and hurt, whether emotional, verbal, physical, sexual, or spiritual.

A partner does not have the right to take away this safe haven through anger, unpredictability, complaining, criticism, the need to control, or any other hurtful behavior. You should not be afraid to be at home. All human beings deserve more than just a roof over their heads; we all need a place to call "home."

This safe haven should be a place to share with friends and family. You don't need to close off your home to the outside world but rather you should have the freedom to invite others in. It is not "a castle" belonging to just one family member who controls how all other family members use the rooms. In order to call it a family home, it needs to be shared equally by the whole family, including you and your children, and your friends.

- **Supported:** You have peace, safety, confidence, and also a place to unwind from the outside world. Friends are welcome in your home.
- **Denied:** You may feel constant stress with no place to be yourself, unwind, and welcome others. Your home may not be predictable or peaceful. Your partner's pessimism may create a negative environment, and constant judgment or criticism may put everything you do under continual scrutiny. You have nowhere to relax or feel safe. You may feel better when your partner isn't home.

YOUR SPACE RESOURCE

Everybody has a right to a certain amount of space in which he or she feels they can control movements and life. When people live together in a house or apartment, they are sharing their lives. However, they still need a small amount of personal space. Some psychologists believe that everyone needs at least three feet of personal space. This space includes room to talk on the telephone without someone listening in on conversations and/or commenting on them. It might mean space to read a book or have a morning cup of coffee without a partner hovering over you. It also includes physical space for personal belongings, mail, books, memorabilia, or whatever someone calls his or her own. Privacy should be guaranteed in this space, and no one else should rifle through this personal space. This space belongs to one person and represents that person's identity. It is not for the judgment of another. The space doesn't have to be big, but it does have to be secure, safe, and private.

- **Supported:** You have room to be yourself.
- **Denied:** You may feel claustrophobic or smothered by your partner.

YOUR SPIRITUALITY RESOURCE

Everyone is born with a spiritual nature and the potential for individual spirituality. A person's spirituality is a way of connecting to the universe, having faith, establishing morals, and expressing beliefs. The spiritual self is present long before one is able to understand religion. Spirituality might be expressed as a part of an organized religion, but it doesn't have to be. The inner spirit of each person has a voice and knowledge of its own; these are not schooled in any particular religious training.

No one can be expected to follow the schedules or standards of any other person or institution. No partner can dictate or define another's spiritual life.

- **Supported:** You have your faith and beliefs to carry you through your relationship.
- **Denied:** You may feel cut off from your source of strength, hope, faith, or direction in life.

YOUR TALENTS OR CAREER RESOURCE

Everybody is born with talents, innate gifts, or abilities. A person's talents might be in business, teaching, parenting, music, art, cooking, hairstyling, athletics, crafts, or anything else. These talents should be allowed to develop for personal fulfillment, as well as for sharing with others.

People have different talents, but that doesn't mean that one talent is better or worse than another. However, it does mean that your partner does not have the right to hold back your talents because of his or her insecurities, lack of knowledge, or need to control you. You need to be able to develop your talents to fulfill your human potential.

In addition, each person in a relationship should have the freedom to choose a job or career (including staying home to take care of the family) that not only fits the needs and goals of the family but also those of the individual.

- **Supported:** You feel you can develop the potential with which you were born.
- **Denied:** You may feel a lack of fulfillment and purpose.

YOUR TIME RESOURCE

Everybody has a right to some personal time. A partner's time doesn't belong to the other partner or the relationship when a relationship begins. You don't lose all your discretionary time when you go into a relationship. Discretionary time gives each individual in a relationship some time in every day or week to choose to do whatever he or she needs, without the demands of satisfying the other person. Everyone deserves this time to release and fulfill personal needs in order to relieve stress and feel whole. This could be time to read a book, go for a walk, watch a favorite TV show, participate in an activity, or visit with friends or family. For a young mother, it could be the chance to take a shower or bath alone without the responsibility of overseeing infants or toddlers. Parents need to share the responsibilities of parenthood so that each parent has some personal time. Partners need to share the responsibilities of the home and daily life so that each person can have some personal time.

Personal time also means we have the right to create our timetable for chores and activities. One partner does not have the right to schedule the other partner. Each person has the responsibility to complete chores in a timely manner without the interference or unsolicited advice of the other partner. Yes, sometimes a couple needs to do and schedule things together, but the partners also need to have the flexibility for give and take.

The personal resource of time allows each person the right to choose how to spend time. Using personal time is not being selfish! A human being's fulfillment in life depends on how well time is balanced among all of a person's responsibilities and interests. No one has a right to dictate that balance and ultimate fulfillment for any other person.

- **Supported:** You have control over your own life and you know it is not selfish to take some time for yourself.
- **Denied:** You may feel your life is at the mercy of your partner and how he or she chooses your time.

SLOW DOWN FOR THIS EXTRA THOUGHT

TIME IS ALL YOU HAVE

Time is one of the most precious gifts you have because it is fleeting.

You can never make up for lost time or lost opportunities. Once the moments have passed, they are gone. So, you must make the most of your time in order to fulfill your dreams, goals, interests, wants, needs, and human potential.

When someone else demands control of your time, that person truly is taking responsibility for fulfillment of your potential and your life. If that person makes mistakes with your time, you lose part of your life— a part that can never happen again.

Be careful of who has control over your time because you will be giving up part of your life.

YOUR YELLOW RIGHTS

Your Yellow Rights are the benefits of being in a relationship.
Both partners mutually share in the responsibilities and
should therefore mutually benefit.

Proceed with CAUTION if you are not receiving your relationship benefits.

Chapter Six

YOUR BENEFIT RIGHTS: YELLOW RIGHTS

CAUTION IF YOU AREN'T RECEIVING ENOUGH RELATIONSHIP BENEFITS

The next color on the traffic light is yellow, and it shows all the added benefits you should gain from being in a relationship. After all, if you can't gain anything from being in a relationship, you might as well stay unattached or live with a roommate. These yellow rights are the reasons most people go into relationships. They represent all the benefits each partner should receive from being in the relationship. Note the important word "*each*".

Proceed with CAUTION if you are not receiving enough benefits from being in a relationship. Both partners deserve these benefits, so a relationship must have give and take for the benefits to be mutual and equal. Neither partner should expect or demand all the relationship benefits at the expense of the other partner. Both partners must support each other's benefits.

YOUR YELLOW RIGHTS ARE:

Acceptance
Acknowledgment
Apologies
Appreciation
Atmosphere
Caring
Cherishing
Commitment
Communication
Companionship
Compromise
Conflict Resolution

Emotional Support
Empathy
Encouragement
Equality
Flexibility
Forgiveness
Friendship
Honesty
Intimacy
Kindness
Love
Mutuality

Optimism
Reliability
Respect
Responsibility Sharing
Sense of Humor
Sensitivity
Sharing
Trust
Understanding
Warmth

Here come the Charming Prince and Fair Princess, again trotting along to Happily-Ever-After, giving each other the well-deserved benefits of their relationship, or so you think.

You imagine they are the perfect loving couple sharing their lives together, both intimately and as friends. You may picture them entwined with each other, laughing, and sharing activities with no arguments or cares in the world. Their warmth and caring radiates from them.

Did it ever occur to you that the Prince might turn to the Princess and say, "This relationship stuff is great, but I don't want to be emotionally involved." Continuing on, he might add, "If you need to get your feelings out, I'll give you a mattress you can bang your head against. But don't expect my support, encouragement, or empathy; you're on your own. Intimacy and honesty, that's questionable. And if you think you'll get reliability, appreciation, commitment, or respect; forget it. As I said, I'll give you a mattress and you can take out all your emotions by jumping or beating on it—but that's all the emotional support I will give you. In addition, the mattress will give you good back support at night!" Or perhaps the Princess gives the Prince a mattress instead.

In either case, the Charming Prince or Fair Princess receives only a mattress for support. There is nothing human or caring. All the emotional support, warmth, encouragement, intimacy, and benefits that occur in a mutually supportive relationship are missing. Although it's hard to think of an uninvolved partner as a mattress, the situation isn't too different from living with an uninvolved roommate. Both a mattress and a roommate give you limited benefits or emotional support, although the mattress might still support your back and the roommate might contribute to the rent, living expenses, or household chores.

Certainly you never dreamt that this Charming Prince and Fair Princess would not be emotionally and/or intimately involved with each other. So how do you recognize this when it is happening in your relationship?

WHY DID YOU ENTER THE RELATIONSHIP IN THE FIRST PLACE?

Your Yellow Rights are the reasons you enter a relationship. They are the benefits you can only receive from being in a relationship. Relationship benefits add value and quality to your life. You can be a wonderfully whole person with just your Green Rights, but the warm feelings and encouragement you get from these relationship benefits motivate you to be in a relationship rather than just being a happy, single person. This is more than the tingling of romance; it is the life benefits you receive from someone you love. So if you thought you were going into a mutually supportive relationship but you're not getting the benefits, then you and your partner need to work harder. And, don't let too many of the benefits wane over time just because of laziness. Keep the benefits coming and the relationship alive. We may grow older but we still need benefits, although they may be shown in different ways.

WHAT DRAWS YOU TO A GOOD LOVE STORY?

Think about your favorite romantic comedy or dramatic love story movie. What makes it so special? Over and over again, it's the same formula. In watching the excitement of a relationship developing on screen, people notice qualities and benefits that they dream of in their own relationship. They watch as trust, communication, friendship, sharing, caring, and intimacy develop between the couple on screen. They identify with the make-believe couple as they make mistakes and laugh as the couple trips over each other and their feelings. Viewers might find tears in their eyes as the couple learns lessons about flexibility, compromise, forgiveness, encouragement, respect, mutuality, sharing, and more, and still their love blooms in spite of everything. People feel warm inside as they leave the movie and might say things such as, "Wasn't that nice!"

Seldom do real-life relationships unfold and evolve like they do on the movie screen, but people still think and talk about what they would love to have in a relationship. The qualities that people talk about after having watched a good love story are the benefits they usually look for in good relationships, the Yellow Rights.

Yellow Rights are the things we can get only by going into a relationship. When people list the things that they want in a relationship, they will usually name the benefits, or these Yellow Rights.

[63]

THINK OF YOUR OWN RELATIONSHIP AS THE LATEST BOX OFFICE HIT!

So now you're strolling down the Relationship Road with your partner, and the movie on the theater marquee is about your relationship. One of the dilemmas in the movie is that one of you receives two tickets to go to a football game and the other has two tickets to go to the theater on the same night. What do you do as a loving couple?

- Do you fight it out?
- Do you each go your separate way with friends?
- Does one of you give back your tickets so that you can accompany the other?
- Do you trade your theater tickets for another night so the two of you can go to the football game together that night and to the theater together at a later date?

As in the above case, everyone's Relationship Road is full of intersections that need to be crossed. At each intersection, one partner or the other must yield to avoid separating or crashing. Both partners must take turns yielding so that both partners can stay on course together.

If you are the only one who is expected to yield and detour, not only will you be held back as an individual, you might also lose track of where you are and why you went into the relationship in the first place. You might get so worried about keeping your partner happy and keeping the relationship together that you forget that you are supposed to receive benefits, too, beyond sharing a roof, taking vacations together, having children, or saying "We're a couple."

ARE YOU RECEIVING ALL YOUR YELLOW RIGHTS FROM YOUR RELATIONSHIP?

If you aren't receiving your Yellow Rights in your relationship, you might need to ask yourself the following questions:

- Why am I in this relationship?
- What was I expecting from this relationship?
- Did I go into the relationship for the right reasons, so that both of us could be enhanced as individuals?

Did you have some other reasons for going into the relationship other than the benefits of Yellow Rights, such as:

- Wanting to be accepted, popular, successful, or "completed?"
- Having children?

- Gaining financial security or care for your physical needs?
- Believing that individuals are supposed to end up as couples?

Truly, none of the above reasons require you to be in a relationship.
- You don't have to be in a relationship to be successful.
- You don't have to be in a relationship to have children.
- You don't have to be in a relationship to take care of your financial security or physical needs.

Going into a relationship for the wrong reasons can cause confusion. It can make you feel bad about yourself and confused about the relationship. So if you appear to have achieved everything you wanted from going into the relationship such as being accepted, having children, and being financially secure but you're still not happy, you might be missing the enhancements of your Yellow Rights.

Even if you went into your relationship for the right reasons, there still might be confusion if you believe that you are the one primarily responsible for keeping the relationship together. In reality, both partners are responsible for keeping the relationship together and for supporting each other's Yellow Rights. Benefits need to be mutual in a healthy relationship.

Your Yellow Rights motivate and justify being in a relationship rather than being unattached. Take a look to see whether you are receiving benefits from your partner. Some benefits might be more important in your relationship than others.

Remember that you don't need Yellow Rights in your relationship to reach your potential as a person. However, if you have those rights, both you and your partner can be enriched as individuals and your life together can be enhanced. The joys of your achievements can be increased by sharing with another.

SOME EXAMPLES OF YELLOW RIGHTS IN RELATIONSHIPS
George & Sophie
When both partners support each other's Yellow Rights, the relationship develops special warmth, comfort, security, and trust that strengthens each partner and the relationship. For example...

Reality Bite...

George and Sophie each had failed marriages behind them. They both were afraid of going into another relationship and thought a new one would be just like their last. But they cared about each other, and before they knew it, they decided to get married again.

Sophie was starting a new job and had children from her prior marriage. She was in financial trouble, as so many divorced women are, but George accepted her with all of her problems and all of her strengths. He encouraged her to do well at her new job and also to take college classes to get an additional degree and further herself. He was always positive and reliable for all situations, whether as a stepparent or a husband. He was warm and took time to be understanding, even though some issues were new to him. Sophie found a new-felt trust and honesty that she had never experienced in her other marriage.

George was going through turmoil in his job, too. He was a CPA whose firm was just merging with another firm. His office was moving into a new location to accommodate both firms. Everyone jockeyed for position. Who would get seniority or the better offices? How many assistants would there be, and who would get them? Offices and files had to be packed up, moved, and reorganized. While his job appeared to be in chaos, Sophie was there to rub George's back, soothe his concerns, and show optimism about the future.

After years of being single, they each had developed personal opinions and styles. Although they were different and had different interests, they respected each other and their differences. This is what seemed to make this new relationship so big and exciting. It wasn't limiting, but inclusive. George and Sophie could be totally honest with each other without the fear of being judged or criticized. They could laugh and share with each other. They were concerned about how they made each other feel. They were quick to apologize when wrong and knew that they would be forgiven and the incident would be over, never to be brought up again. They cherished each other for who they were as individuals and developed an intimacy that neither had ever felt before.

The reality is...

The Yellow Rights helped support George and Sophie in the tough times, expand and share in the good times, and develop an intense warmth, openness, and intimacy all the time. They knew they cherished each other and this made them feel bigger and stronger than single individuals.

Andrea & Jack
Marcy & Adam

When your Yellow Rights are not supported, you might feel as though you could be just as well living with a roommate or a mattress. When your Yellow Rights are not just denied but obstructed, you might feel that living with your partner is like lugging a boat anchor behind you that is stuck in muck. Every effort toward intimacy becomes a major challenge. Although your partner might support your Green Rights, without your Yellow Rights, you might be just as well off alone. At least then you are in control of everything you do. For example...

Reality Bite...

When Andrea and Jack first started dating, they loved to do everything together. They enjoyed going to popular new movies on the weekends and liked being with other couples. Jack was supportive of Andrea's work, and Andrea was supportive of Jack's. However, after several years of marriage, Andrea barely saw Jack, even though they lived under the same roof. When Jack came home from work, he changed clothes, gobbled down dinner, grabbed his six-pack from the refrigerator, and headed into the basement to play with his computer. He went to bed after Andrea was asleep. In the morning when Andrea awoke, Jack had already gone to work. On the weekends he went bowling with his buddies, and Andrea spent her free time alone. When Andrea tried to share her concern, Jack got defensive and left the room without resolution. Andrea felt stuck with nowhere to turn. He wasn't bad to her but he wasn't positive, warm, encouraging, or intimate either.

Jack still loved Andrea, respected her as a separate human being, and encouraged her development. He never tried to control her or deny her any of her Green Rights/Personal Resources. In fact, he was very supportive of all her Green Rights, but still, Andrea might as well have been alone! Other than sharing a roof with Jack, she received few benefits from being in the relationship. They were more like roommates than a couple.

Marcy and Adam lived across the street from Andrea and Jack. Marcy had been the homecoming queen in college, and Adam adored the ground she walked on. Adam worked hard and took on a lot of overtime to be able to buy Marcy the things she wanted. However, after he bought her everything she asked for, she then wanted more. She didn't want to go out and get a job or lift a finger to help. She just wanted to go to her health club, go shopping, and gossip with her girlfriends. She never wanted to go out with Adam anymore. She was always too tired or had a headache. If Marcy did agree to go out one night, it took a major effort that soon became hardly worth the energy. At home, she would start her long beauty routine right after dinner, and then go to sleep. She wouldn't even stay up to talk or be with Adam. Adam felt alone, despite everything he had bought for Marcy.

The reality is...

For Adam and Andrea, the street they lived on was truly "Lonely Street." They both might as well have been living alone. Although they both still had all of their Green Rights/Personal Resources, they received no Yellow Rights/Benefits from being in their relationships. Both of their partners refused to yield to the relationship benefits, the Yellow Rights, that Adam and Andrea deserved. There was no sharing, mutuality, or warmth—just two people living together without being a mutually supportive couple.

Another look...

How these couples would interact if they were supporting each other's Yellow Rights:

Jack cared about how Andrea felt. Although he still came home from work and checked his e-mail messages, he didn't spend too much time on the computer. Instead he would help Andrea fix dinner and wash the dishes later, because they both had worked all day. They spent time at the dinner table and openly communicated and shared their experiences and feelings. They actually started to laugh together and have fun. Jack began to understand that conflicts need resolution and he showed more understanding and appreciation for Andrea. Rather than Jack bowling with only his buddies, Andrea joined a couples' league and they bowled together once a month. On other nights Jack went out with Andrea and her friends. Importantly, now they both cared more about each other and the intimacy in their relationship grew.

Across the street, Marcy lost her self-centeredness and began to support Adam. When she realized how much Adam cared about her and had given her, she was able to appreciate and acknowledge Adam and give him the emotional support and encouragement he needed. They renewed their close friendship and warmth just as they had in college and began doing things they liked together. They truly cherished each other as individuals and showed it through respect and acceptance of each other, both for their strong points as well as their weak points. Their mutuality and intimacy showed how much they cared about each other.

SUMMARY CHARACTERISTICS OF YELLOW RIGHTS

Yellow Rights can give you wonderful relationship benefits:

- *On happy occasions, you can double your joy because there is someone with whom to share it.*
- *In difficult or sad situations, you know someone will support and comfort you.*
- *On a daily basis, you can confide in your partner as a friend and a loyal companion. Your partner is willing to share responsibilities and you can unquestionably rely on this support.*
- *For your challenges and goals, you have someone to encourage you, support you, and offer a positive atmosphere in which to accomplish those challenges.*
- *When you want to have fun and laugh, you can count on someone to laugh with you and not at you.*
- *When you and your partner have differences, you know they will be respected, and conflicts will be resolved in a positive way.*
- *When you have concerns about others, you know in your relationship there is always honesty and trust.*
- *Most of all, you have someone with whom you feel special and intimate. This person cherishes you for who you are and his or her caring and warmth can be felt every day.*

Below are definitions of your Yellow Rights, and a brief description of how you may feel when they are supported or denied by your partner. If you want an expanded description of any of your Yellow Rights, a listing of the different aspects of each right in a relationship, or a more detailed explanation of how you may feel when they are supported or denied, go to www.relationshiprights.com.

ACCEPTANCE BENEFIT

Acceptance means that your partner accepts all of you, including your beliefs that are the same as your partner's and those that are different, your good points and your not-so-good points, your friends, your family, your successes, and your mistakes—all without being judgmental. Your partner accepts you as you are.

- **Supported:** You know that you are loved as a whole person with your good and bad qualities, your successes and mistakes, and with your differences from your partner.
- **Denied:** You may give up or question parts of yourself to make sure you're accepted by the one you love.

ACKNOWLEDGMENT BENEFIT

Acknowledgment means that your partner recognizes your efforts and deeds, whether they are for the relationship, yourself, your partner, or others. It is a positive recognition and is never critical or derogatory. Acknowledgement can be shown verbally or through a physical act of recognition (like a note, a special meal, or flowers).

- **Supported:** You know your partner sees and appreciates your efforts and contributions.
- **Denied:** You may feel your efforts are worthless or that they are done in a vacuum.

GENUINE APOLOGIES BENEFIT

Genuine **apologies** mean that your partner knows how to honestly say "I'm sorry" when he or she makes a mistake or does something to hurt you. Your partner can freely admit when he or she is wrong.

- **Supported:** You know your partner cares more about how you feel than falsely covering his or her own self-pride.
- **Denied:** You may feel like a sponge just sucking in all the hurt and being expected to take it. You never feel safe from your partner's repeating the same actions because your partner has never said he or she was sorry for them. Either your partner doesn't recognize anything is wrong or doesn't care.

APPRECIATION BENEFIT

Appreciation means that your partner recognizes all that you bring to the relationship and is thankful for it. Your partner shows you that he or she appreciates you with kind words, caring gestures, or other types of supportive actions. You and your partner often use "please" and "thank you" even when they are in response to ordinary acts.

- **Supported:** You know that your actions and efforts are recognized by another as special.
- **Denied:** You may feel taken for granted.

POSITIVE ATMOSPHERE BENEFIT

A *positive* **atmosphere** is the result of optimism. It is an atmosphere of encouragement, energy, and positivity. It's a healthy place to live, grow, and be yourself. In this atmosphere, relationships become a nurturing ground for new ideas and successes.

- **Supported:** You are with someone who creates an encouraging support system in which to live.
- **Denied:** You may feel you have no support or that you are drowning in your partner's negativity.

SLOW DOWN FOR THIS EXTRA THOUGHT

REFLECTIONS: WHEN YOUR PARTNER CREATES A POSITIVE ATMOSPHERE

You look forward to waking up and facing your partner. You share your expectations of the day.

You look to your partner as a source of encouragement for your day and your efforts.

As you leave each other, you kiss and say, "Have a great day," and your partner actually means it,

When you get together after work, you share the positive highlights of your day and know you are leaving the problems behind.

You look forward to seeing each other and exchanging your good times of the day.

When you face problems in life, you can count on your partner to raise your spirits

Your partner helps give you positive support to find answers and see the bright side.

Your partner accepts the bad with the good in life, butchooses to focus on the good.

You become a part of your partner's positive energy.

You go to bed at night with a smile on your face and think, "What a nice day."

And you mean it!

CARING BENEFIT

Caring is showing concern for you as a person. Your partner does more than accept you, your partner goes the extra step to show concern for how you feel as a person. Your partner can do this through his or her touch, comments, or actions. Your partner bases his or her caring on your individuality, not just what you give to the relationship.

- **Supported:** You know your partner is concerned about you and supports you unconditionally.
- **Denied:** You may feel that you're not important as an individual and that your feelings don't count to your partner.

CHERISHING BENEFIT

Cherishing is the feeling that comes when your partner treats you as though you are the most unique and special person in the world. Your partner sees you as not only an individual human being but also is someone very special, and those feelings are reflected in the way he or she treats you. Your partner values you and thinks you are precious, and this differentiates you from the millions of other people in the world.

- **Supported:** You know that you are special to your partner and your partner treats you that way.
- **Denied:** You don't feel like you are special to the person you love. You feel like you're just another person on the street to your partner. In fact, your partner may treat others better than you.

COMMITMENT BENEFIT

Commitment is the dedication of a partner to the relationship. In a healthy relationship, the dedication of both partners should match as closely as possible. Whether a partner sees this relationship as short term, long term, exclusive, non-exclusive, or just a trial, both partners ideally are feeling the same level of commitment.

- **Supported:** You have comfort in knowing that your partner is with you in the relationship as far as you want it to go.
- **Denied:** You may live with insecurity or continually have questions about the relationship.

COMMUNICATION BENEFIT

Communication means that partners can communicate freely with unconditional acceptance and without fear of judgment or criticism. You are both accepting listeners and speakers.

- **Supported:** You know you always have someone with whom to share your joys, ideas, thoughts, and concerns without fear of judgment or unsolicited comments.
- **Denied:** You may feel stuffed up inside with no way to communicate. You may think that you're a bad communicator since the communication appears to be one-sided.

COMPANIONSHIP BENEFIT

Companionship means that you and your partner enjoy spending time together regardless of what you are doing. Your partner supports your interests, and he or she enjoys accompanying you. The time you spend together could include attending your favorite activities or just being together for a quiet evening in front of the fireplace. Companionship doesn't mean that you have no space of your own or that your partner has to go everywhere with you. However, it does mean that you can count on your partner to accompany you in a supportive way and without being difficult, critical, or judgmental.

- **Supported:** You know you will always have someone to joyfully accompany you in life without having to beg.
- **Denied:** You may feel alone. Or, when your partner does accompany you, it's like your partner comes with a chip on his or her shoulder.

COMPROMISE BENEFIT

Compromise is your partner's positive ability to meet you partway to settle the differences in your relationship. Both partners give something to achieve a mutually acceptable result. Because a partner gives doesn't mean that he or she has lost. Both you and your partner win by creating a solution.

- **Supported:** You know that your partner will willingly give of him or herself for the sake of the relationship.
- **Denied:** You may feel that you always have to be the one who does all the giving to solve differences in the relationship. When your partner gives even a little toward a compromise, he or she may complain so much that it's easier for you to give everything rather than attempt a compromise.

CONFLICT RESOLUTION BENEFIT

Conflict resolution is the desire and the skill to resolve conflicts amicably. It requires the concern and interest of both partners to solve problems. With conflict resolution, the end result isn't always a winner and a loser. You and your partner desire to end conflicts with a win/win feeling. Neither wants to prolong a conflict or take a conflict to the very end until one partner loses. Sometimes there may be a compromise, but other times there may just be an acceptance of each other's differences.

- **Supported:** You know that conflicts don't always have to end up in a fight with a winner and a loser in order to be resolved.
- **Denied:** You may avoid voicing your concerns because you know how differences will end—either you let yourself lose or the fight goes on until you do.

EMOTIONAL SUPPORT BENEFIT

Emotional support is the comfort and strength your partner gives you in times of emotional need. Your emotions might be ones of joy, love, pride, sadness, fear, anger, grief, or any other emotion. Emotional support can include saying things such as, "I understand," "That's okay," or "I'm so excited for you." Emotional support can also be an action such as a soft touch, a pat on the back, or a trip together to a special place.

- **Supported:** You have comfort and support for your feelings and concerns.
- **Denied:** You may keep your feelings to yourself for fear they will be trampled by your partner or you keep a stiff upper lip, knowing that you can only count on yourself.

EMPATHY BENEFIT

Empathy is the most beautiful way for two people to share feelings. Empathy is your partner's desire to try to feel what you are feeling. Because we are not physically able to put ourselves inside another person to know exactly what he or she is feeling, empathy means that your partner cares about you so much as an individual that he or she tries to understand and share your feelings from your viewpoint.

- **Supported:** You know your partner cares about you as a person from the inside of your thoughts and feelings.
- **Denied:** You may feel distant from your partner, as though your partner has no interest in understanding you.

ENCOURAGEMENT BENEFIT

Encouragement means that your partner not only accepts you but also encourages your efforts, your interests, and your potential to become all that you can be. Your partner is your strong supporter, and you feel motivated.

- **Supported:** You have a cheering section behind all your efforts.
- **Denied:** You may feel left on your own or like you have a "boat anchor" around your legs, hampering your ability to do things and criticizing your efforts.

EQUALITY BENEFIT

Equality means simply that your partner accepts that both of you are individual human beings with human qualities and the same human rights. He or she treats you as an equal with no exceptions. Your partner does not make demands on you as a lesser person or try to control you.

- **Supported:** You know that your individual feelings and personal development are as important to your partner as his or her own.
- **Denied:** You may not feel as human as your partner. Your feelings, talents, interests, etc., are of lesser importance or of no importance at all.

FLEXIBILITY BENEFIT

Flexibility is the ability to adapt and change as necessary without complaints. You and your partner realize that your relationship involves two people, which means that you both need to be flexible in order to accommodate each other's needs. Your partner is able to handle changes in plans or circumstances without getting angry or upset. He or she isn't rigid in expectations of you or others. Flexibility means partners are willing to respect each other's priorities even if that means occasional inconvenience in order to be accommodating. When both partners are flexible, they share the burden of flexibility, accommodate each other, and support each other's needs.

- **Supported:** You are with someone who will help smooth out the bumps in life's road, because every difference or change from a plan can be faced with acceptance and adaptation rather than resistance or commotion.
- **Denied:** Every situation in life with your partner can become a big issue even if it is only a minor problem or change. You may feel that you bend to meet your partner's needs, but your partner can't bend to meet yours.

FORGIVENESS BENEFIT

Forgiveness is the act of excusing somebody for his or her mistakes, shortcomings, or wrongdoings. In relationships, forgiveness has two parts. The first part is your partner's ability to know how to forgive genuinely. It's not a superficial, "Oh, you're forgiven, but..." The second part is to close the door on the subject once it is forgiven. The forgiven act never comes up again, either in conversation or in the heat of an argument.

- **Supported:** You can move forward in life without carrying baggage or guilt from the past.
- **Denied:** Anything you do is subject to your partner's criticism FOREVER. You can never move beyond a mistake—your partner can bring it up again anytime and anywhere.

FRIENDSHIP BENEFIT

Friendship means that you not only have a companion but also someone with whom you can share almost everything—a true friend. Friendship means giving, caring, and sharing your lives together.

- **Supported:** You know you always have your best friend by your side with whom you can have fun and share.
- **Denied:** You lack the closeness of living with your best friend; you may be living with a warm body, but not someone with whom you feel the bond of friendship.

HONESTY BENEFIT

Honesty sets the foundation for your relationship. With it you are able to believe whatever your partner tells you. Your partner is honest about him or herself and displays no false fronts to mask insecurities. Your partner also freely accepts your honesty without threatening punishment or abandonment if he or she doesn't like the truth.

- **Supported:** You have confidence in what your partner says and can share freely.
- **Denied:** You are never sure whether you can believe you partner.

INTIMACY BENEFIT

Intimacy is more than just physical/sexual intimacy; it is a connection of souls. You feel no need for pretenses because you each have the freedom to share your most intimate selves openly, honestly, and with the assurance of total acceptance.

- **Supported:** You can share both physically and emotionally with complete comfort and openness.
- **Denied:** Your partner is not your "soulmate."

KINDNESS BENEFIT

Kindness means being good to each other every day. Kindness is a combination of caring, sharing, sensitivity, and respect. It is shown through caring acts. Kindness cannot just be felt or kept inside; it must be given to someone for it to exist.

- **Supported:** You know that your partner will always treat you with warm feelings and actions.
- **Denied:** You may feel that you are treated harshly or without any concern at all.

LOVE BENEFIT

Love is more than just the words "I love you." Love is also more than a feeling; it is giving of yourself to your partner. Unless someone shows and gives love, no one knows it exists; it's only words. Feeling love, giving love, and connecting love are different things. To have connecting love, both partners freely give of themselves. If one partner isn't capable of selfless giving, then he or she isn't capable of unconditional loving or a mutually supportive relationship.

- **Supported:** Giving in the relationship is mutual. You feel unconditional acceptance, caring, sharing, and concern.
- **Denied:** You may feel confused because your partner says that he or she loves you but doesn't give of him or herself to show it. You may feel that love is a one-way street.

MUTUALITY BENEFIT

Mutuality is a relationship that flows evenly both ways. Both partners give, both partners receive, and both partners grow.

- **Supported:** You know that whatever you give you will also get back, so you feel energized by the mutual exchange.
- **Denied:** You may feel drained, because your partner isn't giving proportionately to the relationship; you do the giving and your partner does the taking.

OPTIMISM BENEFIT

Optimism means looking at the world, your partner, and your family in a positive way. Although problems and shortcomings exist in everything and everyone, they all have good sides, too. Optimists will focus on going forward and looking for solutions, but pessimists will look back, rehash, and be dragged down by dwelling on the problems. Optimism is a choice about how you want to live.

- **Supported:** You know that your partner will keep your spirits up and help encourage you in life.
- **Denied:** You may feel dragged down by having to create optimism for both you and your partner or that you're living in a hole dug by your partner's pessimism.

RELIABILITY BENEFIT

Reliability means that you can count on your partner. You have confidence that your partner will be there for you regardless of the circumstances you might face in your life. Your partner's support is predictable and unconditional, and you don't have to beg for it.

- **Supported:** You feel relief from carrying all the burdens in life because you can count on someone to be there for you.
- **Denied:** You are never sure if your partner will be there for you and you usually need to have back-up plans or go without help.

RESPECT BENEFIT

Respect means that your partner holds you, as an individual person, in high regard. Your partner not only accepts you as a person but also holds you in high esteem. He or she also supports and honors your human rights in the relationship because your partner recognizes them as a part of you.

- **Supported:** You know that you will always be treated with concern for how you feel and what you are as a person (rather than the services you perform).
- **Denied:** You may feel kicked around by your partner or like a person who doesn't matter.

SLOW DOWN FOR THIS EXTRA THOUGHT

11 SIGNS OF RESPECT IN A RELATIONSHIP

A partner:

1. *Listens and cares about your feelings and opinions.*
2. *Accepts when you change your mind.*
3. *Is able to admit being wrong.*
4. *Speaks to you in the same manner and tone that he or she expects from you.*
5. *Supports your friends and your right to have friendships outside your relationship.*
6. *Makes sure that you feel safe when you are together.*
7. *Lets you be yourself.*
8. *Is willing to compromise in order to resolve a conflict.*
9. *Accepts "no" as an answer when you don't want to do something.*
10. *Honors your right to privacy and your possessions.*
11. *Doesn't expect you to be perfect and accepts your mistakes without judgment or punishment.*

RESPONSIBILITY SHARING BENEFIT

Responsibility sharing means you and your partner both take responsibility for things that have to be done, and you work together to accomplish them. If you have children, you each share in the responsibility for their nurturing and caretaking. You and your partner split responsibilities according to abilities and available time rather than by gender or cultural expectations.

- **Supported:** You know your partner will help fulfill responsibilities without concern over whose job it is.
- **Denied:** You may feel like you are filling the lion's share of the responsibilities for the relationship. You help your partner when he or she requests, but help rarely comes your way when you need it.

SENSE OF HUMOR BENEFIT

A **sense of humor** is the spontaneous ability to laugh and look at the humorous side of things. It keeps relationships fun by adding an extra dimension. It gives you and your partner an outlet for relationship needs and stresses.
- **Supported:** You are with someone who can lighten any situation and laugh with you rather than at you.
- **Denied:** Life with your partner always seems heavy and serious; there are no light spots. You may lack outlets to diffuse stress or conflicts between you and your partner.

SENSITIVITY BENEFIT

Sensitivity means that your partner shows his or her concern about your feelings and needs. Your partner might not feel the same things that you do; however, he or she is aware of your feelings and shows consideration and care toward them. Your partner understands and fulfills your needs, whether with support and encouragement or tenderness and silence.
- **Supported:** You can always feel comfortable with your partner, because you can have your guard down and be yourself knowing you will not be hurt by the one you love.
- **Denied:** Your feelings may be hurt regularly by your partner and you may avoid him or her to avoid being hurt.

SHARING BENEFIT

Sharing is the openness of the give-and-take process. When both partners are open, the give-and-take can flow freely. You and your partner can share ideas, feelings, needs, and concerns.
- **Supported:** You know you have someone to be with who will increase the joy of your good times and minimize the effect of troubles in your tough times.
- **Denied:** You may feel you have to carry the burdens of the relationship alone; you're carrying the burdens for two.

TRUST BENEFIT

Trust is knowing that you can count on and believe your partner for what he or she says, does, and will do. Your partner cares about how you feel as a person and therefore acts in ways that support you. Your partner also has the common good of you and the relationship at the center of his or her existence, and you know this will continue in the future.

- **Supported:** You can believe in your partner and this gives you the foundation on which to build a future.
- **Denied:** You may lose faith, reliance, and belief in your partner. You may question your partner's commitment to the future.

UNDERSTANDING BENEFIT

Understanding means that you have a deep and true familiarity with each other. Words are not always necessary. Your partner knows you so well that he or she appreciates how you think and feel. Your partner can anticipate how you might react to a situation because he or she knows the importance of your past experiences and the influence they have had on the person you are today.

- **Supported:** You know your partner comprehends who you are as a person and believes in you.
- **Denied:** You may feel like a stranger to your partner, as if your partner doesn't really know who you are as a person.

WARMTH BENEFIT

Warmth is a cozy, comfortable feeling with your partner. It is a feeling that you can't always put into words: the sense of being surrounded by warm fuzzies and the knowledge that your partner cares deeply about you. It can also be romantic, like lying in front of a warm fire and being comforted or having your back rubbed.

- **Supported:** Your partner creates and shares feelings that give you an inner "glow."
- **Denied:** Your relationship may seem cold or indifferent; you're just a couple and not a pair of lovers.

SLOW DOWN FOR THIS EXTRA THOUGHT

*BEING IN A RELATIONSHIP IS NOT WITHOUT ITS COST,
BUT YOU SHOULD GET EVEN MORE IN RETURN.*

You MUST yield to your partner and give up something of yourself for him or her to gain the benefits of being in a relationship with you. Therefore, being in a relationship will cost you some of yourself, your time, your interests, and more. However, your partner should also be yielding AND giving back to you at the same time. This exchange should create better individuals and a stronger relationship.

This mutual exchange will give you more in return than it costs.

If you are giving of yourself but getting little or nothing back, then your relationship is a one-way ticket with no return trip.

YOUR RED RIGHTS

Red Rights are safety from harmful behaviors that should STOP.

STOP tolerating hurtful behaviors. Your Red Rights tell you that you have a right to be SAFE in your relationship.

Chapter Seven

YOUR SAFETY RIGHTS: RED RIGHTS

STOP TOLERATING HARMFUL BEHAVIORS; YOU SHOULD BE SAFE IN A RELATIONSHIP

The traffic light for your Relationship Rights now turns red. A Red Right is a right to be safe in a relationship. Partners should feel safe from behaviors that hurt and detract from them as individuals. No one has a right to hurt another in a relationship, whether emotionally, psychologically, verbally, sexually, or physically. When your Red Light goes on, you know that these behaviors should STOP!

YOUR RED RIGHTS ARE:
Safety from Accusation and Blame
Safety from irresponsible Anger
Safety from being Assigned Status
Safety from Black-and-White Thinking
Safety from Button Pushing and Brainwashing
Safety from Constant Complaining (or a Negative Environment)
Safety from Control
Safety from Denial and Avoidance

Safety from Discounting and Diverting
Safety from Entitlement
Safety from Humiliation
Safety from Hurtful Physical or Sexual Behaviors
Safety from Indifference
Safety from Judgment and Criticism
Safety from being Ordered
Safety from being a Possession
Safety from Responsibility for Another's Happiness
Safety from Rewriting History
Safety from Shame and Punishment
Safety from Threats
Safety from inappropriate Tone of Voice

Just as there are certain behaviors and activities that you should always do and expect of yourself and your partner, there are also behaviors you should never do or tolerate. Your Red Rights keep you safe from behaviors that are clearly damaging and harmful to you and your human qualities.

Harmful behaviors are not just those things that are physically harmful, but also those that are emotionally and psychologically harmful. These behaviors are destructive, and they hold you back from reaching your full potential and deny your identity as an individual. They violate your human qualities, detract from your ability to function as an individual, and hurt you emotionally and psychologically.

In an unhealthy or confusing relationship, your Red Rights, your safety from harmful behaviors, are often the rights that are overlooked in the evaluation process. If you are not physically hit or abused, everything else is considered okay. Or, when we look at a relationship, we tend to look only at good qualities, and say,
"But my partner is such a good provider."
"But my partner goes to church every Sunday."
"But my partner doesn't smoke or drink."
"But my partner takes such good care of the kids."
"But my partner doesn't cheat on me."

Just because your partner does all of these positive things doesn't necessarily mean that your relationship is good. It's confusing, because there might be other behaviors that can counteract or detract from these. This is why you need your list of Red Rights for validation and to clear any confusion.

Once more, let's check on our dream of the Charming Prince and Fair Princess.

In our dream, they are naturally "lovey dovey." They would never hurt each other, because they care too much how the other feels. Their castle is always safe with no outbursts or unpredictability. They welcome guests in their home with open arms. It is a positive place of optimism and hope, because they take responsibility for their own decisions. They're never afraid of being together, because there is constant respect, support, and empathy between them.

Would you ever expect that the Prince might really be the "Big Bad Wolf" in the Prince's clothing or that the Fair Princess might really be a Shark dressed to look like the Fair Princess? Out in public, the Prince or Fair Princess look like model partners, but at home their real nature might emerge. They might attack and hurt their partners, not necessarily physically, but verbally and emotionally, so that their partners live in fear of setting off their real nature. The partners generally feel crazy and confused because in public they still look like the Charming Prince and Fair Princess, but at home the partners live in fear of the Big Bad Wolf or the Shark coming out. How much should the partners tolerate of the Big Bad Wolf and Shark?

Certainly nobody goes into a relationship to be hurt. But often our partners have a public life and a private life that are totally different. In public, your partner looks like a saint, but in private, you live in fear. We all think we are with the Prince or Fair Princess of our dreams—many couples are. However, if you start to feel hurt, confused, or afraid of your partner, relieved when your partner is away, or live in fear of setting him or her off, then check underneath your partner's clothing and see whom you are really with in your relationship. The Red Rights list will help you determine your partner's real nature.

WHY DO WE TOLERATE HURTFUL BEHAVIORS?

Unfortunately, sometimes when your Red Rights are violated, you become confused and might tolerate harmful behaviors without realizing it. This could happen for a number of reasons:

1. **You Might Tolerate Harmful Behaviors Because You Can't Identify Them by a Name.**

   If your partner hits you, you can easily identify it as harmful and unacceptable behavior. You recognize physical harm as something that you should never have to tolerate. However, you might not be aware that your partner can harm you and your relationship in other less obvious but equally harmful ways. Other emotionally harmful behaviors are often more difficult to identify because you rarely see them listed or named. For example, have you ever seen complaining, criticism, judgment, black-and-white thinking, threats, or rewriting history listed as unacceptable behaviors in a relationship? If you haven't seen them identified as unacceptable, it is difficult to name them as unacceptable. You might feel the effects of the behavior, but without a name or validation, the feeling is hard to understand or explain. Instead, you continue to tolerate things you can't identify.

2. **You Might Tolerate Harmful Behaviors Because Each Incident by Itself Seems Small.**

You might also tolerate harmful behaviors because you are too close to the situation to see the big picture. Each emotional or verbal hurt from your partner might seem insignificant and small. For example, every time your partner gives you an order, calls you a name, criticizes you, raises his or her voice, or refuses to listen to your point of view, it may bother you. But each incident by itself is not significant. At the time, you see and respond to only one incident at a time. However, when the same hurtful behaviors keep coming up incident after incident in slightly different ways, or you start walking on eggshells for fear of setting your partner off, they add up to a bigger picture of a harmful relationship. While each incident is small, the repetitive pattern is harmful, and you might be too close to recognize the bigger picture.

3. **You Might Tolerate Harmful Behaviors Because You Feel It's Your Responsibility to Make Your Partner Happy.**

You might also tolerate harmful behaviors because you believe you are responsible for making your partner happy and keeping the relationship together. But how much hurt should you have to tolerate for the sake of a relationship? How far can your partner go to harm and control you before you say, "This is beyond being supportive. I shouldn't be hurt this much as an individual." Where do you draw the line? Understanding your Red Rights helps you decide where to draw the line on harmful behaviors.

Remember your Partners' Starting Agreement: "Both partners in a relationship are individual human beings who deserve to be treated that way." They each have the same human rights. Both partners in a relationship are adults and are responsible for controlling their behaviors and not harming each other. If your partner doesn't respect your rights, you might regularly live with any or all of these harmful behaviors. But once you know your Red Rights, you will all have names. You will be able to call them your Red Rights, your rights to be safe from harmful behaviors. You will be able to point to the Red Rights in this book, read the definitions and descriptions, and confirm your right to be safe in the relationship. Show this list to your partner if you wish, but most importantly, STOP tolerating the behaviors.

It is important to remember that when a partner respects you as an individual human being, you never have to worry about violations of your Red Rights. This is a person who takes responsibility for the results of his or her actions and realizes he or she has the choice and ability to control their own behavior. This is a partner who respects you and your feelings and does not believe he or she has a right to harm you. Your partner cares about you as an individual and is sensitive to keeping you safe.

RED RIGHTS CARRY MORE WEIGHT THAN GREEN OR YELLOW RIGHTS

When your partner doesn't respect your Red Rights, it is especially harmful and destructive to you as an individual, so Red Rights carry a heavier weight than Green or Yellow Rights.

Violation of Red Rights Is Dangerous—When You Run a Red Light, Someone Might Get Hurt!

When driving in traffic, if you don't obey a green or yellow light, you might end up with a traffic jam, but no one is likely to be physically or emotionally hurt. However, if you don't stop at a red light, you might cause an accident and physical harm. The same goes for your Red Rights. If the harmful behaviors don't stop, you might be hurt physically, emotionally, developmentally, or in all three ways.

Violation of Red Rights Makes You Live in Fear All of the Time

When your Red Rights are violated, you may live in fear all of the time, even though the behavior might happen only a small percentage of the time. You might live in a constant state of being on-guard because you never know when the behavior will erupt or what will cause it to erupt. Your partner might erupt not because of something you have done but because of something that occurred at work or home. You might not be the cause of the eruption, but you, or your family, will be the victim.

Although you might have most of your Green and Yellow Rights in your relationship, suffering from harmful behaviors could totally offset all the personal and beneficial rights. Your Red Rights are immediate STOP SIGNS because they overpower all the rest of your rights.

Violation of Red Rights Can Make You Feel Crazy

Routinely having your Red Rights violated can be confusing. From the inside, the violation is not as clear-cut as it might look to an outsider. Accepted lies masked as truths are part of the violation, and these untruths can make you feel crazy. Just as we couldn't recognize the Big Bad Wolf and the Shark in the Prince and Fair Princess's clothing, Red Right violations are often difficult to recognize because they are masked as something justifiable. If people knew that their Red Rights were being violated at the moment of the violation, they would likely not allow it to happen. But at the time of the incident, the violator makes you feel confused and even crazy. Your partner always seems to know how to defend and justify his or her hurtful action. And rather than your being the victim, your partner twists and justifies the behavior so that you are now the perpetrator.

Often the Red Rights violator justifies the behaviors in such a way that the behaviors appear appropriate and you are the one who is at fault. You are made to believe that you are responsible for the violation of your own rights. How does this happen? Unfortunately it's all too easy. The violator takes a grain of truth from you and expands it to justify his or her whole action. The little grain of truth gets twisted into a big lie.

For example, in the case of the Big Bad Wolf, when he starts verbally, emotionally or physically attacking the real Fair Princess, he might use a small incident like burning his toast to justify his hurtful actions. He might say, "You burned the toast, so you deserved to be attacked." The Fair Princess knows that she burned the toast, but she also knows that it was an accident and that it wasn't so serious. She didn't burn the house down, although the kitchen did smell for a while and she had to open the windows to air it out. But what she doesn't realize is that being attacked in any way isn't an acceptable reaction to burnt toast. Or, maybe the Big Bad Wolf verbally or emotionally attacked her because dinner was late, she didn't pick up something at the store, the house wasn't cleaned, or she got a speeding ticket on her way home. Whatever the incident, nobody ever deserves to be attacked in any way in a relationship. The Fair Princess did not make the real Big Bad Wolf come out of the Prince's clothing to attack her. The Prince just didn't respect the Fair Princess enough to control his own actions.

However, the Big Bad Wolf and Shark are smart and wily and know just how to twist their actions to make them appear justifiable. The Big Bad Wolf in this case said to the Fair Princess, "If you hadn't burned the toast, everything would have been fine." All of which is probably true.

So in the end, the Fair Princess might be the one to apologize to the Big Bad Wolf, and she might accept the Wolf's attack as justifiable behavior.

Unfortunately, when the Fair Princess is so close to the incident, all she can do is smell the burnt toast. She doesn't realize the truth—attacks of any sort, whether an angry temper, punishment, name-calling, shaming, or hurtful actions, are not justifiable for any reason.

In real life, when situations like this occur, it is very confusing. You may feel crazy, because you don't understand why you deserve this treatment, yet you recognize that you may have burnt some toast or done something wrong. You need to step back and look at the big picture to see what is really happening.

1) Step back and look at the whole situation. Realize that your partner doesn't have a right to hurt you no matter what you do.

2) Separate the lie from the truth.

3) Acknowledge the truth to your partner and apologize if appropriate.

4) Tell your partner that he or she doesn't have a right to yell at you, punish, you or hurt you no matter what you did.

In the case of the Fair Princess burning the toast:

She would have recognized that the Prince did not have a right to yell at her or attack her in any way, despite her burning the toast. And then she would have said to the Prince:

"I'm sorry for burning the toast, but that doesn't make it right for you to yell at me or attack me. You don't have a right to hurt me, no matter what happened. STOP!"

Even if the Prince does not stop his yelling, the Princess realizes that she is not at fault and did not cause her partner's behavior. She will realize that she is living with someone who does not respect or acknowledge her Red Rights as an individual. She can see her relationship more clearly.

Do not be apologetic for your partner's abusive behaviors; don't feel that they are justified or that you caused them.

Recognize the confusion and apologize for your actions, but tell your partner that your actions do not justify his or her hurtful behaviors and they must stop.

We all want to believe that we are loved by our partners, that our partners care about how we feel and won't hurt us. Unfortunately, the truth is: that most Red Rights violations happen because our partners do not care how we feel. They are more concerned about justifying their actions than how they hurt us.

Having Your Red Rights Doesn't Mean Your Partner Has to Be Perfect

No one can expect a partner to be perfect. Every once in a while people lose their tempers, say things they shouldn't, or lose control of themselves, even in healthy relationships. However, in healthy relationships, violating partners recognize their hurtful actions and apologize. They don't blame you or try to justify their behaviors. In healthy relationships, partners work out their differences with positive resolutions, and you don't live in fear of hurtful behaviors recurring frequently. When you, or your family, lose your Red Rights, you regularly live in fear of an eruption of harmful behaviors from your partner. If you live in fear or feel like you are walking on eggshells, then you know your Red Rights are being violated.

Certainly anything that physically hurts you should never be tolerated. However, your Red Rights include safety from emotionally and developmentally harmful behaviors that can give you warning signs before any physical harm occurs. Your Red Rights include verbal and emotional violations prevalent in our culture. But most of us are not aware that these actions can be far more damaging than physical abuse. Physical wounds usually heal, but scars from emotional abuse linger in our minds.

SOME EXAMPLES OF RED RIGHTS IN RELATIONSHIPS

Recognizing Red Rights violations in relationships might not be as easy as it sounds. The key word here is the recognizing, not the violating. If your partner physically hits you, it is easy to recognize that as a harmful violation. However, verbal and emotional violations are not as easy to identify. Take a look at these couples and see what happened to them.

Barbara & Bart
When you don't know your Red Rights by name, you might find them difficult to identify.

Reality Bite...

Barbara and Bart had been married for ten years when they went to a marriage counselor. Barbara was feeling that something had been wrong with their marriage and wanted help, but she couldn't put her feelings into words. While they were in a session together with the counselor, Barbara shared a concern, saying, "I'm afraid of Bart."

The counselor then asked her, "What are you afraid of?"

The room was silent as Barbara thought about how to answer the question.

But she couldn't explain her feelings. Finally she responded, "I'm afraid he's going to leave me," which was one of the threats Bart often used when he wanted to get his way.

The counselor smirked and asked her, "Well, has he ever left you?"

Barbara had to say, "No."

The counselor chided her, "Then what are you really afraid of?"

The counselor and Bart then laughed at her for how foolish she sounded.

Bart then stopped going to the counselor because it appeared that he was doing nothing wrong and his threats were acceptable behavior for relationships. However, Barbara continued to go, because she still felt that something was wrong with the relationship. In one of her last sessions alone with the counselor, Barbara asked him what she should do about Bart's hurtful behaviors. He told her that she had to accept Bart as he was. The counselor put it to her, "Bart isn't going to change, so you have to learn to live with Bart as he is, or you should leave." She felt confused, as though she was the one with the problem and was making mountains out of mole hills. She stayed in the relationship another seven years and accepted Bart's abusive behaviors. She felt frustrated and gained eighty pounds in one year because she didn't know where else to turn. So she continued to tolerate the hurt and control, because she had no way to identify Bart's behaviors as unacceptable and had no basis to question the professional.

The lie used to justify Bart's threats:
When Bart didn't want Barbara to do something, he would threaten to leave the relationship. Barbara believed she was responsible for pleasing her husband and certainly she didn't want to do anything that was so serious to make him leave. Then it would be her fault that they got divorced due to her being a bad, selfish wife. So Barbara would cancel her plans to avoid the threat of Bart's leaving. She believed Bart when he said her plans would hurt him so much that he would leave. And, importantly, she believed the counselor, who told her that Bart wasn't doing anything wrong and she just needed to accept him as he was.

The truth about Bart's threats:
Bart used threats to control Barbara and her life. He had no plans to leave, but Barbara didn't know this and shouldn't have had to risk it. Barbara believed her husband, as wives should be able to do. Once Bart learned that threats worked to control Barbara, the number of threats escalated, and he used threats on such small things as whether she could take the children to a dog show, whether their

child could invite other kids over to play outside on a snow day, or whether she could take a cooking class with her friends (after she had already enrolled and paid the money).

The truth is, Bart's threats were a manipulation of Barbara's trust. Bart didn't respect her as a separate person and was more concerned about maintaining his control over her plans than how she felt. If Bart had cared about Barbara, he would have accepted her as a separate person worthy and capable of making her own plans and doing things that were important to her. He would not have felt the right to dictate what she should and shouldn't do or control her plans through threats. If Barbara's plans meant so much to Bart, he would have had the integrity to discuss his serious concerns rather than resort to threats or bluffs in order to get his way.

The reality is...

Barbara finally divorced Bart.

The counselor had inappropriately supported Bart's immature bullying and threats as unacceptable means of communication between partners. He then made light of the fact that Bart had no plans to ever follow through with his bluffs and was actually lying and threatening in order to get his way. The counselor then insinuated that Barbara was naive and immature to be so trusting of her partner as to actually believe what he said. How silly of her to believe her husband!

However, five years after divorcing Bart, Barbara read this book and saw the list of her Red Rights. She was then able to say to Bart, "I was afraid of your threats, your screaming, your anger, your blaming, your criticizing, your shaming, your black-and-white attitude, your constant complaining, your punching holes in the wall, and finally I was afraid that one day you might cross the line and physically hit me."

With that, Barbara could finally name her fears and know that she had been justified in divorcing Bart. She had a right to be free from hurtful physical or verbal behaviors.

(The marriage counselor is probably still sitting in his office telling some other unwitting person or couple the same harmful advice to tolerate hurtful behaviors because he or she can't name them.)

Bart, unfortunately is in a new relationship and still doesn't know that his hurtful behaviors are unacceptable. And since he is still unaware, he has no relationship with his child either.

Another look...

If Bart, Barbara, and the marriage counselor had communicated honestly and fairly:

When Bart and Barbara went to a marriage counselor, the marriage counselor had the knowledge and integrity to tell Bart that threats of any kind are an inappropriate means of honest and fair communication with his wife. He told Bart that when he threatened Barbara, he was disrespectful and hurtful. She was not trying to control him by making a decision; she was just trying to be herself. The counselor then asked Barbara to describe what it felt like when Bart threatened her. He helped Barbara to explain her feelings to Bart. Did it make her crazy to think that Bart would equate her going to a cooking class with a divorce? Did she really believe that Bart would leave? Did she want to risk it over a cooking class or a dog show? He then needed to ask Bart why he made the threats. The counselor told Bart that although he might not want to go to a cooking class himself, think that his wife was too fat, or that she shouldn't spend time cooking for him, he had no right to expect to control his wife and everything she did. He then went on to say that threats made Barbara live in fear of making any plans because she never knew which incident would cause him to leave— so she eventually stopped making plans of any kind because of his continual threats of leaving.

Finally, the marriage counselor said to Barbara, "Because you can't change somebody doesn't mean his or her behaviors aren't hurtful and wrong. It especially doesn't mean you should stay in the relationship, accept them, tolerate them, and continue to allow yourself and your child to be hurt by them."

After more counseling, Bart no longer threatened Barbara. He loved and respected her as a separate person and didn't want to stoop to such hurtful tactics as threats with someone he loved. Instead of using threats to impose his will, he shared his thoughts, rationale, and persuasive powers. After listening to Bart, Barbara had the final decision and Bart accepted it as right for Barbara, although it might not have been the same decision for him.

Or,

If the couple had seen a list of Red Rights, Barbara would have been able to identify and name Bart's hurtful behaviors and explain to him that his threats and other actions were unacceptable, regardless of whatever the counselor said. But without the list, Bart could justify his actions and Barbara had nothing to validate her feelings. A list of Red Rights would have helped Bart and Barbara recognize their situation sooner. They could have either corrected the behaviors and saved their marriage or stopped the hurtful situation from dragging on so long.

Sheila & Bob
Daily negative communication is hard to identify as abusive, because it is so regular that you learn to adapt and live with it as though it is normal.

Reality Bite...

Sheila and Bob were regular church-goers who both sang in the choir. Sheila had a part-time job in a nursing home where she worked with the elderly, and to the church and outsiders, she seemed like the most caring wife and mother. Bob worked in a local factory. All their friends in the choir thought they had a great relationship. But in their home, things were different. Sheila didn't know how to say anything without yelling. She would constantly shout orders and commands to Bob and their kids. When something went wrong or the family members didn't obey, then her anger would escalate and the yelling, screaming, name calling, and accusations would really heat up. She might do this in front of Bob's or the kids' friends and totally humiliate them. Her kids didn't want her to come to school to help with anything because they were afraid of being embarrassed by her yelling. All Sheila could do was complain. Her family rarely heard a compliment or a positive statement. Nothing was ever good enough, no matter how hard everyone tried. When Bob came home, she would immediately begin interrogating him, as though Bob had no time of his own. He had to report all of his activities to Sheila. When she wanted something done, all she could do was nag. When she was done nagging, she'd nag again. Bob worked hard and tried to please her. He loved her but stayed at work later and later to avoid being with her. He felt this was just the way women were and this was how married life was supposed to be. Still, everyone in church thought they were the perfect couple.

The lie Sheila used to justify her complaining:

Sheila told Bob she had a right to share her feelings, whether complaining or anger. This was just the way she shared, and he had to accept her as she was. Bob shouldn't keep secrets from her, so she had a right to interrogate him about everything. When she gave orders or nagged, she claimed these were things that had to be done around the house. Sheila said her comments were truthful and honest; she wasn't lying, so she wasn't doing anything wrong.

The truth about Sheila's behavior:

No one has a right to verbally hurt another person, even if it seems like everyday conversation. However, words don't always become hurtful because of what they say but for how they are said. Sheila never listened to herself nor did she have to take responsibility for what she said or how it came out. Her family did not deserve to be barraged with her yelling, negativity, orders, complaining, or nagging. She put her family constantly on the defensive and under a negative cloud. Her family had a hard time living under these hurtful circumstances and couldn't conduct their lives in positive ways. Sheila pounded her family's self-esteem into the ground and took no responsibility for the results of her actions. They just had to learn to deal with her mouth.

The reality is...

After their last child left home, Bob had a hard time continuing to take Sheila's verbal pounding. He had to take it all by himself because no one else was around for her to yell at. Bob stayed later and later at work or went out with the guys before coming home to face Sheila. The more he stayed away to avoid the yelling, the worse Sheila got when he was home. Sheila finally went to a counselor and complained about Bob coming home late and her being home alone. The counselor would only meet with Sheila, so she heard only Sheila's side of the story. She had no understanding of what living with Sheila was really like. So, the counselor agreed with Sheila. She told her that Bob should be home and not stay out so late after work. She reaffirmed Sheila's feelings based solely on what Sheila told her, never knowing what home was like for Bob. After receiving confirmation of her feelings from the counselor, Sheila divorced Bob.

Bob felt bad about the divorce. He truly loved Sheila and never expected a divorce, but the first night he was alone, much to his surprise, he felt free, relieved, and released. He felt wonderful. The dark cloud that Sheila had always hung over his head was finally lifted, and he had room to breathe and smile. He realized that the world wasn't a negative place. Other people communicated with him without yelling. People actually said "Please," rather than giving him orders, and then "Thank you" to show they appreciated him. Bob knew that he didn't have to live as he had for the past twenty five years of his marriage, and he realized that he had learned to adapt and never knew that Sheila's verbal behaviors were abusive.

Sheila was finally alone and had to listen to herself complain. She had no one to help her with chores or order around. Her kids never came to visit for fear of having to listen to her complain and interrogate them about Bob. Instead, they visited their father who was understanding, warm, and comforting, as a parent should be.

Another look...

If Sheila had communicated by showing respect to Bob and caring about how she made him feel:

Sheila grew up in a home where yelling, ordering, nagging, and complaining were everyday occurrences, but she didn't like it. Instead of repeating the behavior, Sheila realized that she didn't have to continue this way of communicating in her own marriage. She took the time to think about what she said and how she said it. She became a positive, supportive wife and mother. Bob appreciated how she acknowledged and respected him. They shared plans and feelings in a positive way. When the kids left home, they came back often to visit.

Or,

When Sheila went to a counselor to discuss some of her issues, the counselor did not make a family judgment without meeting the family. The counselor asked to talk to Bob and other family members without Sheila present in order to get a full picture and at least hear both sides before making a judgment. The counselor was then able to help Sheila with her problems rather than blame the family and tell Sheila to get a divorce. With the counselor's help, Sheila was able to get past her childhood problems without carrying them on to another generation. Sheila and Bob were able to keep their family happily together.

Paula & Chad
Each incident by itself might seem small, but if the incidents are daily or frequent, they can add up to one big on-going hurt.

Reality Bite...

Paula and Chad went to the same church as Bob and Sheila. They lived in their home with their three children ages two, five, and eight. Chad was a good provider and a regular churchgoer, he was faithful to Paula, he didn't smoke or drink, and he said he was concerned about the kids. However...

- Every time the phone rang and Paula answered, Chad would hover over her to listen into her conversation or even yell at her until she hung up. He complained and got angry that Paula's friends were calling and taking her time away from him.
- As soon as Chad came home, his nightly rant at Paula was, "Where's dinner?" even though Paula worked too and got home from work at about the same time as Chad.
- Regularly Chad would yell at Paula, who might be in another room or in the middle of an activity with their children, "Where are my socks?" or

shoes, shirts, papers, or whatever he was too lazy to look for at the time. It was Paula's responsibility to keep track of all of his belongings and drop everything in response to his call.

- Whenever Chad was home, he yelled at Paula, "Can't you keep the kids quiet?" The children were not allowed to be children while Chad was home. He expected the children to be pint-sized adults, and this was Paula's responsibility.
- Chad continually complained, "The house is always a mess." Chad would never lift a finger around the house; it was Paula's duty to put away all of Chad's papers, clothes, dishes, and anything else he messed up, as well as take care of the kids.
- Each night when Chad came home from work, the sofa, which seated four, was off limits to everyone else. There was certainly enough furniture in the room for the whole family, except that Chad sprawled out over the entire sofa so that the rest of the family had to fight over the one remaining uncomfortable chair in the room or sit on the floor. If one of the kids tried to stake out a little piece of the sofa, everyone got a lecture about how Dad had earned the right to the sofa all for himself because he worked all day (even though Paula did too). Paula usually sat on the floor with the kids.
- Every time the family sat down to dinner, Chad snapped at the children's table manners. He could never seem to say anything nice at the table. Finally, family meals became totally unpleasant.
- Every time Paula had to go to a company outing, Chad was unhappy. This year, Chad grabbed Paula tightly by the arm, announced gruffly in front of her boss that they were leaving, and pulled her toward the exit. Chad yelled at Paula all the way home for spending too much time at the party with her boss and his wife.

When Paula and Chad went to marriage counseling and she was asked to describe her relationship with Chad, all that Paula could name were Chad's good qualities as she described at the beginning. All of the other incidents listed above seemed small and petty, so she didn't mention them at first. In fact, she felt a little silly mentioning them at all.

She repeatedly questioned herself, "Are any of these incidents alone worthy of ending my relationship? Do I want to start a fight over the whereabouts of my partner's socks, who should sit on the couch, or a ringing telephone? Do I know anyone who would choose to end a relationship because of their children's table manners, someone yelling, 'What's for dinner?', or 'Can't you keep the kids quiet?' Or because someone hogged the sofa?" Would any single one of these incidents be so harmful or destructive to warrant ending a relationship?

The lie Chad used to justify his treatment of Paula (and his family):

Chad was a good person. He went to church every Sunday. He didn't beat his wife. He wasn't an alcoholic or a cheater. He went to work every day, made sure the rent was paid, and put food on the table. A wife shouldn't expect more than that. As long as he fulfilled his responsibilities, he could treat his family however he wanted. Paula was just being petty.

The truth about Chad's attitude:

All the incidents mentioned above were small and individually hardly even worth discussing, except that they represented Chad's attitude toward Paula and the rest of the family. He didn't view them as equal human beings. Somehow they were lesser than him. They were not worthy of space to talk on the phone, to sit on the sofa, to be spoken to in a respectful manner, to be helped with household chores or dinner, or to attend company functions without being criticized. The incidents themselves might have been "small potatoes" in terms of the whole relationship, but Chad's attitude toward Paula was "BIG POTATOES."

This attitude was the motivation behind treating her and the children with such low regard. His behaviors showed a pattern of assigning status, ordering, complaining, blaming, controlling, irresponsible anger, criticism, name calling, and responsibility for another's happiness. This pattern revealed Chad's harmful and degrading treatment of Paula as an individual.

Chad had some good qualities, but they didn't give him the right to treat Paula and the children like second-class citizens. Bad behaviors never have to be tolerated, no matter how big or small, and no matter how many other good qualities a person might have.

The reality is...

Paula finally broke into tears after one of those small incidents. She couldn't take it anymore but didn't understand what her problem was. It wasn't the small incidents—the socks, the dinner, or the sofa. Her problem was the feeling she had about herself in the relationship. She and Chad went to a marriage counselor who came highly recommended by their pastor. After several sessions, both alone and together, the marriage counselor pointed out Chad's hurtful behavior pattern and attitude toward Paula as a lower class human being. Chad was never conscious of his attitude or took time to realize how he was treating Paula and the kids. He had focused only on himself, never meaning to hurt them. The counselor then told them that having some major good points does not justify all the other hurtful and degrading behaviors.

They are still working on their marriage and Chad is trying to change his attitude toward Paula and the children. Things are looking good for their relationship.

Another look...

If Chad had a respectful view of Paula as an equal human being:

Not only would Chad go to church on Sunday and be a good person, but Chad also would...

- Give Paula space on the phone when she wanted to talk to her friends.
- Share responsibilities for preparing dinner because they both worked the same hours and came home around the same time each day.
- Take responsibility for keeping track of his own belongings, putting his own belongings away, and keeping the house clean.
- Treat the children with respect and not expect them to act like adults.
- Share the sofa and other furniture with the family as equal members of the family. The house belonged to all of them, not just Chad.
- Make dinner a time where the family would look forward to being together.
- Support Paula's job in a positive way whether at company outings or other required duties.

And most importantly, he would respect Paula as a separate and equal human being.

Nick & Nora

Often the violator takes a grain of truth about an incident and expands it into a lie to justify his or her whole behavior. This can be confusing; the violator claims that he or she is the victim. Then the real victim ends up apologizing to the violator. Confusing, isn't it? It's even worse if you are the victim.

Reality Bite...

One morning Nora offered to cook Nick a big breakfast. Nick wanted bacon and two fried eggs, over easy. Nick went into the kitchen to keep Nora company while she was cooking. As Nora was frying the eggs, she broke one yolk. Nora didn't think too much of it because she had broken many other yolks before in her life, and nobody seemed any worse for it. However, this time before the egg's yellow liquid even began to ooze into the white center, Nick grabbed the pan from her, physically pushed her away from the stove, and started yelling at her. "Give it to me; I'll do it myself" he said. "I told you not to turn it so soon. You never do anything I tell you." Nick took over the cooking while he continued to yell at Nora.

When he was finished cooking, he grabbed Nora by the upper arm, shoved out a chair, and pushed her into it at the kitchen table. Then he slid the plate with the broken yolk in front of her and continued screaming, "Now you eat it!" As he pulled up a chair for himself and sat across from Nora, he ate the two eggs with unbroken yolks.

Nora was shaking and scared to death. She didn't know what he was going to do next. Nick and Nora's five-year-old daughter was afraid and started crying hysterically; she didn't know what terrible thing her mother had done in order to create her father's loud and violent behavior.

When Nora asked Nick to stop yelling, it only got worse, and he made fun of her cooking and again reprimanded her for not following his directions. Nick told her that his behavior was her fault; she deserved it. After all, Nora did this to herself by breaking the yolk. Nick continued his self-righteous indignation by giving Nora the silent treatment for the rest of the day. Nora ended up apologizing profusely for the whole incident. She felt hurt—and crazy. Was she really wrong? Did she really deserve this behavior? How was she supposed to know when her Red Rights were being violated when she knew she was at fault for starting the incident, as innocently as it might have began?

The lie Nick used to justify his yelling, screaming, blaming, pushing, and grabbing Nora:
Nick accused Nora of breaking the egg yolk, which she did. He then said he was angry because she broke the egg yolk, and if she hadn't done it, nothing would have happened. This is probably also true. Nick told Nora that the whole incident was her fault, and she started it when she broke the yolk.

The truth about Nick and Nora's actions:
Although it is true that Nora broke the egg yolk, Nick had no right to react as he did. Breaking the yolk was an accident and it hurt nobody. Yelling, screaming, grabbing, and shoving were Nick's violent, hurtful reactions that should have been controlled. Nora didn't make him do any of those things. A mature, responsible, caring partner can learn to control himself or herself. No one ever has a right to hurt his or her partner with violent acts under any circumstances. Nick further compounded the hurt by blaming Nora for making him do it. Now she was not only feeling afraid and hurt but also crazy. Nora was not the perpetrator. She should not have had to apologize to Nick for his hurtful behaviors. Nick's behavior should not have been tolerated for any reason.

The reality is...

Nick was able to twist the truth, to make Nora believe that his behavior was appropriate and that she was wrong. He became the victim, and Nora the perpetrator. Nora really had accidentally broken the yolk; that was the grain of truth. It was not the first time a yolk was ever broken. However, Nick expanded on Nora's accident and erupted violently, as though the broken yolk justified his behavior—that was the lie. The result was that Nick's behavior became acceptable, and Nora's wasn't. Nora felt crazy.

After that time, she was afraid to fry an egg for Nick—they were all either scrambled or hard-boiled. Worse than that, Nora and her daughter were extremely cautious around Nick for fear of setting off the next incident. Would it be a neglected dust ball? An untimely telephone call? A toy that wasn't picked up? Or an undercooked meatball in the spaghetti sauce?

Another Look

If Nick had taken responsibility for his actions and had the self-control to handle his reactions:

While Nick might have been unhappy that Nora broke the yolk, he would have realized that he had alternative choices rather than reacting as he did. In life, yolks break, milk spills, things get lost, cars get dented, and Nick would have realized that at all times he had choices as to how to react. When the yolk broke, instead of reacting as he did, Nick might have said:

- "It's okay, there are two eggs; the other one isn't broken."
- "I don't mind if one is broken; they all taste the same."
- "There are more eggs in the refrigerator. Let's just get another one."
- They could have both laughed and said, "Let's have some scrambled eggs!"

Or

- Even though Nick did lose his temper when the yolk broke, after he cooled down, he could have apologized to Nora for his behavior. He would have recognized he was wrong and apologized for hurting Nora. Nora would have accepted his apology and life could have gone on with mutual respect.

Another Look

If Nora had recognized the violation at the time of the broken yolk and the yelling:

Nora would have known that while she accidentally broke the egg yolk, the mistake did not give Nick the right to react as he did. She was not responsible for Nick's behavior, nor did she create it. He was responsible for his own self-control. Instead, she would have confronted Nick and said, "I'm sorry that I broke the yolk, but that does not justify your yelling, screaming, and pushing me. This is abusive. STOP!"

Max & Stephanie
Supporting Red Rights means partners choose to control themselves rather than their partners.

Reality Bite...

Stephanie came home from the grocery store and took her toddler out of his car seat and into the house along with all the bags of groceries. When she finished unloading the groceries, she realized that she had left her purse in the grocery cart with her wallet in it. She had put her keys in her pocket as she loaded the car, but left her purse under the cart when she drove off. She was hysterical and upset when she realized what she had done. She immediately called the store and asked them if someone had found her purse and turned it in; the customer service desk said that no purses were there. She packed up her toddler and drove back to the store to look, but couldn't find her purse under any of the carts. Someone had found her purse with her wallet and taken it with all her money, identification, and credit cards inside. She drove home feeling angry about leaving her purse and even madder about the person who took it without turning it in.

Stephanie's husband Max came home shortly after Stephanie came back from the store the second time. When Stephanie told him what had happened, he was furious. He felt angry at Stephanie for being so careless. All he could think about was someone using the credit cards, stealing Stephanie's identity, and ruining their lives. While Max felt very angry, he also knew how angry and upset Stephanie was too. Just at that moment their toddler started crying and begging for dinner, which was now late. Showing his anger and yelling or scolding Stephanie was not going to solve the problem. Hitting their toddler and telling him to shut up would mean nothing to the toddler, because a one-year-old knew nothing about lost wallets, credit cards, or identity theft. One-year-olds only know that it is past dinnertime. Max knew that he needed a few moments to get in control of himself. He told Stephanie that he needed to take a drive and asked her if she could start feeding their toddler and looking up the phone numbers of the credit card companies to cancel the cards.

Max realized that he had a choice about how he wanted to act and needed time to think.

As Max drove around the block he thought about punishing Stephanie by taking all of her credit cards away, making her call all the credit card companies to straighten out their problems, and reprimanding her for creating these problems. However, he then remembered several months before when he had been backing out of the garage as he was talking on his cell phone and hit the side of the garage with the car. He damaged not only the car, but also the garage. Stephanie had warned him many times before about his not paying attention when he was on his cell phone and here he had damaged both the car and the garage doing just that. When Stephanie came out of the house after she heard the crash, she didn't yell at Max and say "I told you so." Instead, when he got out of the car, she gave him a hug and said "Accidents happen." She had arranged for carpools for herself and their toddler, so that Max could use her car while his was being repaired.

Max respected Stephanie and didn't have to lie to justify his actions, because he knew he could control his actions.
Max drove back to the house after driving around the block. He realized that showing his anger would only hurt Stephanie and not help solve the problem, although he was angry at the dishonesty of whoever took the purse. When Max got home he helped fix dinner and afterward made all the calls to the credit card companies to notify them of Stephanie's lost wallet. He helped soothe Stephanie's nerves and reassured her that "Accidents happen" and that everything would be okay.

The reality is...
Max and Stephanie accept that they will each make mistakes. Neither feels the right to punish or reprimand the other when "accidents happen." Yes, they both may feel angry at times, but they both realize they have a responsibility to control how they show their anger and how they treat each other.

SUMMARY CHARACTERISTICS OF RED RIGHTS

If you have your Red Rights:

- *Your partner respects you as a separate person and he or she will rarely violate your Red Rights.*
- *When you hit bumps in the road, your partner knows how to get back on course.*
- *When your partner has a problem, he or she takes responsibility for his or her actions.*
- *When you make a mistake, your partner accepts it as a part of life rather than a deliberate act or as an incident deserving punishment.*
- *Your partner accepts you rather than expects to control you or be your superior.*
- *Your partner is flexible and accepting rather than rigid and unaccepting.*
- *Your partner accepts your differences as your identity rather than flaws.*

- *You never have to live in fear of your partner's actions. You do not have to live in an on-guard state or feel the need to walk on eggshells.*
- *You can be totally open and comfortable with your partner despite your differences.*
- *When you and your partner have differences, you don't feel crazy or question your reality.*
- *Your partner cares about how you feel and won't act in ways that hurt you, despite his or her feelings.*
- *Red Rights are your protection from being hurt in a relationship.*
- *When you have your Red Rights, you're safe!*
- *When you have your Red Rights, you are free to be yourself.*

If your partner violates your Red Rights:
- *Your partner will likely violate whichever rights are necessary to get his or her way, because he or she doesn't care about how you feel.*
- *When your partner or relationship hits bumps in the road, your partner may blow them out of proportion because your partner doesn't know how to accept them and has difficulty getting back on track.*
- *When you make a mistake or an accident happens, you can usually anticipate your partner's punishment or criticism. To your partner, mistakes and accidents are not acceptable in life (except when your partner makes the mistake).*
- *You might often feel crazy or off-balance because your partner might use fear rather than rationality or respect to make his or her point.*
- *You might feel like an inferior being or possession rather than an equal human being.*
- *You might feel that trying to succeed in anything isn't worth the struggle because your partner might tell you that the worst will always happen or that you are no good.*
- *Your partner might tell you that you are responsible for all the problems in the relationship because he or she can do nothing wrong.*
- *You might feel that if you just did things better, you could fix the relationship.*

- *You might feel that if you just did as your partner ordered, he or she would treat you better.*
- *You might just accept the hurt rather than question or fight it because questioning or resisting your partner only makes your partner's actions worse. Tolerating the hurt might be less painful than fighting it.*
- *You might just accept your partner's statements and opinions although you disagree because you know your partner is inflexible. Nothing you say will change his or her mind or encourage acceptance of your differences.*
- *You might try to avoid your partner as much as possible because that minimizes your exposure to confrontation or hurt.*
- *When you don't have one Red Right, you usually don't have most of your Red Rights, because your partner doesn't respect you or your feelings as an individual.*

Below are definitions of your Red Rights and a brief description of how you may feel when they are supported or denied by your partner. The definitions also describe a **general truth** and the **possible partner's lie** that make a violation of a Red Right so confusing at the time. A look at the **big picture** describes how the behavior might look if you take a step back. If you want an expanded description of any of your Red Rights, a listing of the different aspects of each right in a relationship, or a more detailed explanation of how you may feel when they are supported or denied, go to www.relationshiprights.com.

ACCUSATION AND BLAME

Accusation and blame mean that one partner accuses or blames another for his or her actions. Your partner would accuse you of causing your partner's behavior toward you or problems in the relationship. Since you are the cause of the problems, you are told you can fix them. You're told that you can change your partner's behavior toward you by how you act and what you do. The partner doesn't take responsibility for his or her own actions. Additionally, the blaming partner might not believe in mistakes or accidents—he or she must always blame someone for everything, even if it's no one's fault. Your partner always acts the part of the victim. Common examples of accusation and blame are statements such as:

"You made me do it."

"You deserved it."

"Can't you do anything right? I'm tired of hearing you say 'I'm sorry.'"

"If you hadn't done this, I wouldn't have done that."

"It's always your fault. What's the matter with you"?

"If you would just do this better, I would treat you better."

Accusation and blame in a relationship are attempts to shift responsibility for one partner's behavior to another. Your partner always has an excuse.

A General Truth: Incidents happen.

A Partner's Lie: Your partner has a right to accuse or blame you for any incident, regardless of what really happened.

The Big Picture: Accusation and blame don't undo an incident or solve a problem, regardless of who or what caused it. Accusation and blame hurt and degrade. They make any incident worse than it already is.

- **Supported:** You have the confidence to know that your partner doesn't always need to find blame for everything that happens in life and is willing to accept responsibility for his or her own actions, if applicable.
- **Denied:** You fear anything that happens in your relationship because you know that your partner will likely blame you whether or not you had anything to do with it. Your partner doesn't accept mistakes or accidents, believing there has to be blame for everything.

IRRESPONSIBLE ANGER

Irresponsible **Anger** is free floating and likely to erupt at any time. It is an uncontrolled reaction or rage by a partner who doesn't think he or she has the responsibility to control his or her actions. Your partner's anger and actions are in excess of the scale of the event. The anger or actions are hurtful or punitive. Your partner might also use tones of voice or gestures and emotions that result in hurt or fear. The anger might be in wild bursts or its remnants (reminders of the event) can extend long beyond the life of the event and can be carried on into the rest of the day, weeks, or even months.

Your partner doesn't take responsibility for the effects his or her actions have on you. Your partner doesn't apologize for overreacting or losing control of his or her anger. You are blamed for making your partner angry, and therefore you are usually the one who is left apologizing for the incident.

A General Truth: People feel anger at times.

A Partner's Lie: Your partner has a right to express feelings however he or she wants. Your partner has no responsibility for controlling anger, because it's an honest expression of feelings. If your partner is angry, your partner can show anger regardless of how it affects others.

The Big Picture: Even though your partner feels angry, your partner still has a responsibility for controlling how he or she expresses it. Your partner doesn't have the right to hurt you through expressions of feelings or anger.

- **Supported:** You have the ability to live in peace, without the fear of setting your partner off or being the brunt of rage.
- **Denied:** You live in fear of your partner all the time, even though your partner isn't angry all the time. Since you never know when the anger will erupt or what will set it off, you always live in an on-guard state.

SLOW DOWN FOR THIS EXTRA THOUGHT

WHEN YOU LIVE WITH AN ANGRY PARTNER, YOUR LIFE ALWAYS REVOLVES AROUND THE ANGER.

A person who exhibits irresponsible anger forces a partner to live in constant fear. Although your partner might show anger only 10 percent of the time, the anger can come without warning 100 percent of the time. Since you never know when the anger will erupt, you may always live in fear of your partner.

ASSIGNED STATUS

Being **assigned status** means that you are assigned a status lower than your partner. Your humanness is not equal. For some undetermined reason, your partner's human qualities are at a higher value than yours. For example, your partner's feelings might be at a higher value, his or her opinions and taste might count but yours don't, your home might be his or her safe haven but not yours, his or her time might be of greater importance than yours. In general, your partner's personal resources and human rights are valued by him or her more than yours.

A General Truth: You love your partner and want to please him or her.

A Partner's Lie: Your partner believes he or she is the master of the relationship and can therefore treat you as he or she pleases.

The Big Picture: Both partners in the relationship are worthy of the same respect and treatment.

- **Supported:** You feel good about yourself and know that you will be able to develop as a whole person.
- **Denied:** You feel like you are a lesser human being or a possession. Your self-esteem is diminished.

BLACK AND WHITE THINKING

Black-and-white thinking is the self-centered, insecure, and narrow-minded belief that subjectivity does not exist in this world—that things can only be done in one right way and questions have only one correct answer. Amazingly, the black-and-white thinker is the only one who knows what is right. Things must be done his or her way or not at all. When questioned, the black-and-white thinker will argue that everything in this world is black-and-white or right-and-wrong. Other answers, opinions, solutions, gradations, or degrees don't exist. The black-and-white thinker doesn't accept any one else's experiences, feelings, situations, beliefs, or knowledge. He or she has difficulty showing compassion, understanding, tolerance, flexibility, empathy, or compromise.

Black-and-white thinkers might also have trouble differentiating whether something is different, slightly wrong, or totally wrong. There is no such thing as a big or little problem; being very late or a few minutes late; or a big accident or a little accident. Degrees don't exist; everything is at one end of the continuum or the other. In fact, black-and-white thinkers don't use a continuum. They consider anything that is different or slightly wrong to be totally wrong. If your partner tells you "It's my way or the highway," that's the sign of a black-and-white thinker.

Black-and-white thinking is one of the most hurtful of the Red Rights because it is the foundation for every single one of a partner's other relationship rights. If your partner believes he or she has the only answers for everything, your rights don't exist. There is no way to have your rights accepted or tolerated. Both partners end up being unhappy; the black-and-white thinker is unhappy seeing you as constantly wrong, and you are unhappy because you are made to believe that something is wrong with you.

An artist once said while driving through the prairie, "Look at all the many shades of green." A black-and-white thinker doesn't see any green; he or she sees only black or white. He or she sees the world through a black-and-white lens, and even then it is still missing all the shades of gray.

A General Truth: There are often multiple alternatives to situations, different opinions on topics, and different tastes, and more than one solution to a problem.

A Partner's Lie: Your partner believes he or she has the best (and only) answers and viewpoints.

The Big Picture: Unless it is a historical, scientific, or mathematical question with only one right answer, most issues have subjective or multiple alternatives. Your solutions and tastes are just as important and worthy of consideration as your partner's. And when serious or minor situations happen, your partner has a responsibility to differentiate between the two and react accordingly. You shouldn't have to face extreme reactions to small incidents.

- **Supported:** You know that your partner recognizes there are numerous alternatives to most situations. Your partner does not always have to get his or her own way or have the only correct answer or opinion. Your thoughts and feelings are respected.

- **Denied:** You feel cut off from communication with your partner and you question yourself, because you know that anything different from your partner's thinking won't be considered. You may fear your partner's reactions to anything, because regardless of how serious or minor the situation, your partner's reactions may be extreme.

BUTTON PUSHING AND BRAINWASHING

Button pushing and brainwashing are forms of manipulation that your partner might use to control you. A button-pusher uses your standards of personal character, your values, or other sensitive issues that you have shared within the intimacy of your relationship in order to manipulate you. Your partner pushes your button by using his or her intimate knowledge of you. He or she might accuse you of doing something or being something that he or she knows will hurt you in order to elicit the desired response.

Some common button-pushing statements are:

"You're not a good partner."

"You're a bad mother/father."

"You're emasculating me."

"You don't care about me."

"You're just like your mother/father."

When your partner pushes your buttons, you react strongly in order to prove that the statement is false. When you are in the midst of a button-pushing situation, you don't realize that your partner is using these statements only to get you to do whatever he or she wants at that time.

Brainwashing can occur over time when your partner repeatedly pushes the same button and "hooks" you until you are ultimately convinced that what he or she said about you is true. After button pushing has occurred so many times, your partner becomes so convincing that you stop defending yourself. You are then brainwashed and actually believe your partner's button-pushing statements.

A General Truth: We all have sensitive issues and concerns.

A Partner's Lie: Your partner believes he or she has a right to use those sensitivities however he or she wants.

The Big Picture: While you want to be open and share your sensitivities with your partner, your partner has no right to use this intimacy to hurt you. Your partner is misusing this knowledge and your feelings to manipulate you.

- **Supported:** You have peace knowing that your partner will not use his or her intimate knowledge for manipulation.
- **Denied:** You question your own sensitivities and thinking because your partner manipulates them to control you.

CONSTANT COMPLAINING

A **constant complainer** grumbles or is negative about anything and everything. Besides complaining about you, your partner can complain about friends, family, health, work, neighbors, politics, the problems of the world, or anything else in the universe. The complainer rarely looks at the good things or works toward solutions.

The complaining can take the form of nagging, badgering, complaining, yelling, interrogating, criticizing, or yapping. The complainer can be a hypochondriac. There is very little peace around your home. A complainer can't say anything nice; everything is bad. In fact, if something is good, you probably WON'T hear about it.

The result of continual complaining is the creation of a negative environment in a household, and the complainer forces his or her family to live under its cloud. The family must continually respond and answer the complaints. With no positive reinforcement, your energy is constantly drained.

A General Truth: There is always good and bad in the world, problems and solutions, and highs and lows.

A Partner's Lie: Your partner says that he or she is just telling the truth about the problems.

The Big Picture: While there is negative in the world, there is also positive to offset it. You've a right to protect your energy from being regularly drained by your partner's distorted, unbalanced, negative view of life.

- **Supported:** You have energy for yourself and important relationship needs, without being wasted on unnecessary complaints and ailments.
- **Denied:** You may feel tired, because constantly having to respond and answer to complaints can wear you out. Every morning when you wake up, you may feel that you will be facing a pile of complaints before you can even start your day. You're tired before your day even starts.

SLOW DOWN FOR THIS EXTRA THOUGHT

REFLECTIONS: WHEN YOUR PARTNER IS A CONSTANT COMPLAINER

You dread waking up in the morning
    Because you feel you are loaded down with the complainer's problems before even getting out of bed.

You look forward to leaving the complainer in the morning
    Because you know this may be the only positive time you have during the day.

You avoid sharing your thoughts with the complainer
    Because the complainer will take your good times down and make any problems worse than they are.

You dread getting back together with a complainer after work or a long day
Because you know you will hear about the same problems with no attempts to solve or deal with them.

You dread handling problems with a complainer
Because you know the complainer would rather complain than work toward a solution.

Even though there are both positives and negatives in life,
You know the complainer will suck all the positive energy out of you in order to deal with his or her negatives.

When you turn off the light to go to bed at night you think,
"Whew, finally I don't have to listen to the complainer and I can have some peace!"

CONTROL

Control happens when one partner directs the other partner's actions and thoughts through any chosen means. A partner tells you what you should believe, what you should do, and what you should not do with all or part of your time.

Your partner might control you through demands and/or giving orders. Sometimes your partner might control you indirectly through fear and threats. Or, you may gladly obey because you want to please your partner, since part of being in a relationship is making your partner happy—but your partner abuses this by requiring control.

Control in a relationship can vary in size and strength. It can be very small and include only a portion of your relationship, such as losing control of Sunday afternoons or the color scheme in your house. Or it can permeate all of your relationship, including both the time when you are together and the time you are apart. The control can be light and suggestive, but when it is strong and fearful, you become afraid of being physically or emotionally hurt or abandoned if you disobey.

A General Truth: You may feel it is your relationship responsibility to help and please your partner.

A Partner's Lie: Your partner believes it is your role to do whatever he or she says in order to please, no matter how controlling the demands. Your partner feels that pleasing him or her means taking possession and control of your life. If you're not submissive to your partner's control, then you're bad and may be accused of trying to control your partner.

The Big Picture: While you want to please your partner, you're still an individual with your own intelligence and needs. You're not a servant or a slave. Your partner has no right to expect control over you.

- **Supported:** You have the freedom to develop as a person.
- **Denied:** You may feel like you are in a harness or on a leash. You may feel unvalued as a person, like an indentured servant under the control of another. You may give up your reasons for living, because you have no control over your own decisions or your own life.

DENIAL AND AVOIDANCE

Denial occurs when your partner verbally rejects the existence of a problem or situation. Ultimately this might lead to the denial of your reality and the eventual shut-down of communication between you and your partner.

Avoidance is a nonverbal form of denial. It takes place when your partner physically or emotionally separates himself or herself from you. It can take the form of the silent treatment, whether you are both in the same room and refuse to talk or your partner leaves and goes elsewhere to avoid a problem or discussion. Avoidance can also happen when your partner increases involvement in activities that keep him or her away from home. These activities might be as simple as working longer or participating in outside interests.

A General Truth: Everyone has a right to his or her own opinions.

A Partner's Lie: Your partner believes he or she has the right to an opinion about the existence of real situations, rather than accept the fact that the situations exist.

The Big Picture: Open communication is important for a two-way relationship. When your partner won't admit the existence of situations or face up to them, your communication is shut off on one end. It's like talking to yourself.

- **Supported:** You know that concerns and problems can be solved together.
- **Denied:** You question your rationality because your partner refuses to recognize any of the concerns you are feeling.

DISCOUNTING AND DIVERTING

Discounting is minimizing or trivializing your feelings or concerns. Discounting can be done with verbal put-downs or through the refusal to discuss something.

Diverting is a form of discounting. A partner diverts when he or she deliberately changes the subject in order to avoid facing a discussion of your concerns.

A General Truth: Your partner does not necessarily have the same feelings, opinions, and concerns as you. Therefore your partner may not understand your feelings and thoughts or have the same reactions to situations as you do.

A Partner's Lie: Your partner believes that since he or she doesn't have the same feelings or thoughts as you, he or she can belittle or deny them.

The Big Picture: No matter what your partner wants to admit or not, your feelings and thoughts are real. If your partner cares about you, your partner will want you to be able to share these so they can be addressed or solved together. Denial does not make issues or concerns go away; it just makes them build up bigger inside of you.

- **Supported:** You know your partner will always respect and listen to your concerns.
- **Denied:** You feel small and/or crazy because your partner treats your concerns as though they are not real or of any importance.

ENTITLEMENT

Entitlement is a partner's belief that he or she is better or more important than you in the relationship and therefore deserving of special rights and privileges. Entitlement may show itself through your partner's selfish focus on his or her own needs, enforcement of his or her own standards and opinions (which are either slanted toward your partner or double standards, but are definitely not mutually agreed upon), and seeing you as a personal possession. Your partner may be unreasonably demanding and rigid; have high expectations of catering or caregiving; become enraged or punitive when inconvenienced or not catered to; upset when children cause you to be less attentive to him or her; angry when children are noisy, messy, or bothersome; furious if you will not sacrifice your needs to accommodate him or her; or make you responsible for his or her feelings or neediness. Entitlement causes your partner to view your attempts to defend yourself and your own needs as neglect or abuse of him or her.

A General Truth: You care about your partner and want to please him or her. You don't want to feel you are doing something wrong to displease or hurt your partner.

A Partner's Lie: You must do as your partner says and respond to all your partner's demands (no matter how controlling, unreasonable, extreme, or hurtful they are) to make him or her happy or else you are branded as a bad partner.

The Big Picture: While you do not want to displease your partner, your partner cannot use undue demands to control you under the guise of displeasing or being a bad partner. Your needs are just as worthy of satisfaction as your partner's.

- **Supported:** You know that you will always be respected as a separate individual with your own needs considered an important part of the relationship.
- **Denied:** You are constantly at your partner's beck and call regardless of your own needs. Your own needs go unfulfilled for fear of being called a bad partner or arousing your partner's anger at not responding as your partner demands.

HUMILIATION

Humiliation can be caused by name calling, jokes that devalue, or being forced into situations that belittle you. Your partner might make you the brunt of jokes. Name calling can include calling you unliked nicknames, saying you are dumb or an idiot, or using obscenities such as "bitch", "bastard", or worse. Jokes that devalue can be those that make light of sensitive areas such as your body, or they can also be jokes made about you in front of others. Typically, when your partner sees that the behavior bothers you, the behavior escalates and occurs more often. When you object, your partner often belittles you and accuses you of being overly sensitive or a prude. Over time, the behavior might become expected.

A General Truth: We all have sensitivities and often face embarrassing situations.

A Partner's Lie: Your partner believes that since your situations and embarrassing areas are real, he or she can do anything with them, regardless of how you feel. He or she can make fun of you in front of others or put you in awkward situations.

The Big Picture: While your sensitivities are true facts, your partner has a responsibility to treat you with respect. Your partner doesn't have a right to make you feel badly or make fun of you without your permission. That's not funny—it hurts.

- **Supported:** You know that your partner cares enough about your feelings that your partner will never make fun of you to hurt you.
- **Denied:** You fear your partner's comments and jokes because your partner thinks it's funny when he or she humiliates you.

HURTFUL PHYSICAL OR SEXUAL BEHAVIORS

Hurtful physical or sexual acts means being pushed, hit, grabbed, kicked, or being the victim of any kind of a forceful, coercive action including forced sex. However, it also means *the threat* of any hurtful behaviors, either to yourself or others, such as children, pets, or personal objects. This includes physically breaking, kicking, or hitting other objects to make you fear that these same violent behaviors could be done to you as well.

A General Truth: We all have a right to our own feelings and their expression in healthy ways.

A Partner's Lie: Your partner believes he or she has a right to express feelings in any physical way he or she wants. Your partner may see this as a means of getting a point across.

The Big Picture: While your partner has a right to express his or her feelings and get points across, your partner doesn't have a right to hurt or threaten you in order to do so. Your partner has other choices of expressing him or herself in non-violent ways.

- **Supported:** You have peace knowing that you will not be hurt in any physical way by your partner.
- **Denied:** You live in constant fear of your partner because you know he or she may hurt you or your possessions at any time.

INDIFFERENCE

Indifference is simply a partner's lack of interest. By itself, indifference is not wrong. Indifference is not hurtful unless you are in a relationship. Indifference can be difficult to recognize because it isn't necessarily intentional. One single event is not an indicator of indifference; a pattern of disinterest and lack of participation in the relationship creates it. Your partner shows a lack of curiosity and interest regarding your activities or feelings and doesn't acknowledge or support your true relationship needs. Many of your Yellow Rights Benefits are usually lacking, but your partner isn't hurting you as an individual. On the outside it might appear that your relationship has everything, but on the inside it feels empty.

A General Truth: Your partner isn't doing anything to hurt you as an individual. Your partner may even be financially providing for you or taking care of the family or the home.

A Partner's Lie: As long as your partner isn't doing anything to hurt you, your partner is doing a good job.

The Big Picture: It takes more than providing services or an absence of hurt to make a relationship. There must also be benefits. When there is a shortage of benefits in a relationship, the relationship hurts or feels hollow.

- **Supported:** You know that you and your relationship will always be special and a priority to your partner.
- **Denied:** You feel alone or that you could just as well be living with a roommate.

JUDGMENT AND CRITICISM

Judgment and criticism occur when you are always subject to your partner's questioning, judging, and comments. Rather than being accepted as an equal partner, everything about you is fair game for your partner's interrogation, judgment, and criticism. Nothing about you is free from comment, even if nothing is wrong. Your partner may judge what you do, what you say, what you buy, and what you wear as well as critique your family, friends, interests, and work. Nothing anyone does is good enough to be free from criticism, no matter how good it is. Your partner is looking for something wrong and will usually find something wrong. Differences are not accepted free from comment and judging.

A General Truth: We all have different opinions, tastes, and assessments of situations.

A Partner's Lie: Your partner believes he or she has a right to express his or her opinions and assessment of everything you do.

The Big Picture: While your partner has a right to his or her own thoughts about what you do, you're different from your partner and deserve acceptance as an individual. Your partner has a responsibility to respect your actions and opinions as right for you. Your partner doesn't have a right to critique you. You can make decisions for yourself without having to face or answer your partner's comments.

- **Supported:** You have the comfort to act freely and be yourself, knowing that your partner accepts you, regardless of what your partner may think.
- **Denied:** You feel unaccepted for who you are. You may avoid telling your partner things because you know that anything you say or do is subject to your partner's judgment or criticism. You're often afraid to make mistakes or to be yourself, so you do as little as possible or tell your partner only what he or she wants to hear.

BEING ORDERED (RATHER THAN BEING ASKED RESPECTFULLY)

Being ordered rather than being asked respectfully means that someone gives commands or demands. A person who orders does not treat others as human beings who have feelings or opinions. Often a tone of voice or physical gesture can make the difference between whether a person orders or asks. Simply using the word "Please" or adding "Would you mind doing...?" is all that is needed to make a person feel respected rather than a servant.

A General Truth: Partners help and support each other.

A Partner's Lie: Your partner believes he or she can command you to help or support whatever he or she wants without asking or regardless of anything else you are doing.

The Big Picture: While you want to help and support your partner, you're still an individual and not a robot or servant. It is your choice to help your partner.

- **Supported:** You know that you are respected as an individual and will always be asked and spoken to as an important person.
- **Denied:** You feel like a child being told what to do by a parent or a boss at work. It makes you feel small or like a worker ant reporting to the head of the hill.

BEING A POSSESSION

Being a possession, rather than a separate, living, breathing human being, indicates that your partner thinks he or she owns you. When you become a partner, you become a possession. You are an extension of that person. You might be a trophy, a toy, a servant, a breadwinner, or anything your partner needs. Your role is to serve him or her. Your partner might claim bragging rights for your activities and accomplishments as though your partner did them him or herself. You are not a separate human being in your partner's eyes.

A General Truth: When people go into relationships, they expect to give their partners benefits for being in the relationship with them.

A Partner's Lie: Your partner expects you to give him or her everything with no regard for yourself.

The Big Picture: Both you and your partner are individuals in the relationship. While you want to give your partner benefits, you should not have to sacrifice your own needs, interests, and benefits in the process. You deserve to maintain your own identity and not just as a possession of another person. A loving partner wants you to be the best you can be as an individual and not a servant.

- **Supported:** You are respected as a separate individual with the ability to make your own decisions and achieve your full potential as a person.
- **Denied:** You feel like a servant or a robot whose only role in life is to provide services for your partner. Your talents, interests, potential, and balance in life are of little or no importance to your partner so you feel unsatisfied and your partner wonders why.

RESPONSIBILTY FOR ANOTHER'S HAPPINESS

Responsibility for another's happiness occurs when your partner puts the burden of his or her happiness on you. Normally we think we are responsible for our own happiness and to some extent for that of our dependent children, but not for our adult partner. However, in this case, your partner shifts the burden of fulfilling his or her life and happiness onto you.

A General Truth: People want to see their partners happy.

A Partner's Lie: Since you agreed to be in the relationship, your partner believes it is your responsibility to make him or her happy. If he or she isn't happy, it's your job to fix it.

The Big Picture: We are all individuals with choices in our lives. Only your partner can make him or herself happy through his or her attitude (optimist or pessimist, problem-solver or complainer, etc.) and his or her actions (active or complacent).

- **Supported:** You are free from guilt for your partner's unhappiness or dissatisfaction; your partner takes responsibility for his or her own decisions for happiness.
- **Denied:** You feel that it's your duty to "complete" your partner because your partner makes his or her well-being and satisfaction your responsibility.

REWRITING HISTORY

Rewriting history happens when your partner changes the facts of a situation. The history can be exaggerated, downplayed, twisted, denied, or outright lied about to cover all or part of an incident. In whichever way the rewriting is accomplished, the end result is that the facts of an incident are not as you remembered them. Rewriting history usually happens only when the couple is alone and when no one else is around to validate the facts. Your partner usually does this to justify and cover up his or her mistakes or wrongdoings. Rewriting history is insidious to a relationship because it is an attack on your mind. When rewriting history occurs over and over again, it eventually causes you to question or doubt your actions, sanity, or the reality of what you see, say, or do. Most of all, you believe you have lost your memory.

Common expressions heard from partners who rewrite history are:

"You never gave it to me."

"You never told me about it."

"I never said that."

"I never did that."

"I did too ask you to do it. You just don't remember."

"That's not what happened. You never get the story straight."

"You're just imagining things."

"You have a bad memory."

A General Truth: Our recollection is only as good as our memory.

A Partner's Lie: Your partner believes he or she can change the facts about incidents that happened in order to fit his or her own needs and then accuse you of having a bad memory.

The Big Picture: While we all have periodic memory lapses, your mind is good. You can remember what you saw, heard, or did. Your partner doesn't have a right to play games with your memory by trying to change or alter facts. Your partner must accept reality and not change it, even if the facts aren't favorable to your partner.

- **Supported:** You have confidence, knowing that you and your partner will tell the same story about incidents, your life, and the relationship.
- **Denied:** You feel crazy and question your own sanity because your partner readily changes the truth in order to fit his or her own self-image or cover for insecurities.

SHAME AND PUNISHMENT

Shame and punishment are deliberate acts of degradation. Shaming is verbal degradation. Punishment is active degradation.

Shaming demeans and puts guilt on a person through accusations such as "bad girl," "bad boy," or "You're good for nothing." This verbal whipping or scolding can leave a person in more tears than a physical beating. Shaming might happen in front of other people who have nothing to do with the situation.

Punishment might be either an act of physical violence such as being hit or an act of isolation or deprivation such as being grounded or having something of value taken away for a period of time.

A General Truth: No one is perfect. Sometimes we do things wrong, make mistakes, or have accidents.

A Partner's Lie: When something goes wrong, your partner has the right to punish you.

The Big Picture: Both partners are adults and neither is perfect. You know when you do something wrong without your partner shaming or punishing you. You are not a child to be disciplined by a parent or a criminal in a court system. Your partner is not your judge and penal system. Mistakes and accidents happen as a natural part of life and should be accepted that way by both partners.

- **Supported:** You know that you will be treated as an equal to your partner. Although you may make mistakes, your partner doesn't feel the superiority to shame or punish you.
- **Denied:** You feel like a child or criminal in front of a parent or a judge. You may feel forced to lie if the truth isn't something your partner wants to hear for fear of punishment. It creates a dishonest relationship and one based on fear rather than respect.

THREATS

Threats are statements of implied enforcement. The threatening partner says that if you do this or if you don't do that, he or she will cause something unpleasant to happen. The threat could be one of physical force. It could be denial of a necessity or something that you like. Or it could be a refusal to do something. In any case, the threatened act will cause pain, inconvenience, discomfort, or emotional distress.

A General Truth: Two individuals will have differences of opinion.

A Partner's Lie: If you don't agree with your partner's decisions, your partner has the right to threaten you until you agree to follow his or her decision. Your partner believes his or her decisions are superior to yours and can threaten any actions to enforce decisions.

The Big Picture: Since two individuals will often have two different opinions, both opinions deserve respect. If your partner wants you to do something differently, your partner should discuss the rationale with you respectfully. Using threats is never an acceptable form of communication, because threats block communication. You have no opportunity to be heard or else you will be hurt in some way. You trust your partner and therefore believe your partner will follow through with his or her threats. Your partner is misusing your trust in him or her in order to manipulate you.

- **Supported:** You know that what your partner says is what your partner does and that he or she will not intimidate you in order to manipulate you.
- **Denied:** You fear your partner and feel forced to do as he or she says, even though he or she may have no intention of following through with the threat. You dare not disobey your partner for fear of the threat happening.

INAPPROPRIATE TONE OF VOICE (OR LOOK)

An **inappropriate tone of voice** means that your partner uses his or her tone of voice to convey a hurtful meaning far beyond the words used. The tone can be loud, scary, hurtful, alarmist, demanding, screaming, harried, or pushy. It can also be whiney, nagging, or any other tone conveying an unspoken meaning. Constant questioning is also inappropriate in a relationship of respect and trust. The tone of voice is meant to exert additional power or control over you. A loud, mean voice conveys, "If you don't do as I say, you will pay in some way." A whiny or questioning voice implies, "If you don't do as I ask, I'll keep nagging or harassing you." An inappropriate tone of voice may be one of the most commonly abused rights, because it can instill fear without raising a hand. Or your partner can have a "crazed" look on his or her face that instills fear without even uttering a word.

A General Truth: People want to be respected by their partners.

A Partner's Lie: Your partner believes he or she can speak to you in any way he or she wants to make you *respect* and respond to him or her.

The Big Picture: Using an inappropriate tone of voice doesn't make you respect your partner. You may respond, but it is out of fear or disgust, not respect. Any communication that is motivated by fear is inappropriate and one-sided.

- **Supported:** You know that your partner is conscious of how he or she speaks to you and respects your feelings.
- **Denied:** You respond to your partner out of fear or nausea rather than respect. You may do things to avoid being with your partner.

PART TWO

WHERE ARE YOU IN YOUR RELATIONSHIP?

YOUR RELATIONSHIP REALITY CHECK

Chapter Eight

YOUR RELATIONSHIP GUIDE

Bill of Relationship Rights

Guidebooks abound, but where are they taking you? Guidebooks can take you to cities for $10 a day, $50 a day or $500 a day. It all depends on your budget. You'd better know your budget before you follow the guide or you may be broke by the end of the tour. Guidebooks include different sections for easy reference like places to shop, eat, or stay. If they weren't divided into topical sections, they would be hard to use with massive listings of places all jumbled together. Descriptions of each listing help you decide which places are more important to you on your trip. Guidebooks are a complete reference source on the topic.

What about Relationship Guides? As we listed in Chapter Two, there are different types of relationships. Before you let anyone guide you in a relationship, you and your partner must first determine the type of relationship you want. Do you want a relationship of convenience? A ruling relationship with a ruler and a submissive partner? An enmeshed relationship where neither partner is whole though they are always together? Or do you want a mutually supportive relationship where both partners are whole individuals and bring more to the relationship to share with each other?

Often partners don't want the same type of relationship, but don't realize it until they are married. People aren't told there are different types of relationships. They assume that when they fall in love, all relationships are the same. It isn't until problems arise in communication that differences are noticeable. Sometimes the relationship during the courtship is different than after marriage. One or both partners may change their expectations without telling the other after the vows are said. During the courtship, the couple may have a mutually supportive relationship and after the wedding, one partner may expect it to change to a ruling relationship without telling the other. It is important that you and your partner agree on the type of relationship you want to have.

Relationship Rights (and wrongs) is for couples who believe "Both partners are individual human beings and deserve to be treated that way." If you can't agree with this statement and/or don't believe your partner will accept it, this is not the guidebook for you. However, if you want this starting agreement with your partner and a mutually supportive relationship, read on. Both partners are treated equally with respect and dignity. Both partners are encouraged to develop and share with each other. Both partners help each other and give to each other. Neither partner controls nor dictates to the other. This relationship is healthy for the growth and dignity of both partners.

A ruling relationship with a controller and a submissive partner can look very compatible, as can an enmeshed relationship. However, neither of these relationships is healthy and supportive for both partners. A relationship of convenience can be healthy, but there is no commitment to mutual support or relationship benefits. So while relationships may look compatible, it doesn't necessarily mean they are healthy or respectful to both of the partners. Many people may have grown up seeing ruling, enmeshed, or convenience relationships as role models. If both partners grow up with the same expectation, these relationships can last and be very compatible. But if one partner decides he or she wants to be treated with respect as a separate individual or wants more relationship benefits, it's hard for these relationships to last. Partners must realize these relationships work only as long as both partners accept their terms. People deserve to learn alternative models for relationships. They do not have to accept the only one they know, especially if it is not healthy for the individual.

Relationship Rights (and wrongs) is a guidebook for mutually supportive relationships.

- It includes a contract for both partners as to how they will treat each other.
- It lists the common elements found in mutually supportive relationships to use as a guideline and benchmarks for your own.
- It divides the elements into three easily recognizable categories associated with the colors of a traffic light to make them instinctive.
- It lists all of these elements together in their respective categories on one page in the Bill of Relationship Rights—Your Relationship Guide for easy reference.
- It gives definitions for each right so that both partners have the same understanding and meaning.
- It gives you a measuring scale to determine where you are with each of your rights in your relationship, both positively and negatively.
- It shows you the rights that are supported and those that need work in order to improve your relationship.
- It gives you the language to communicate with your partner, pointing to specific rights to help explain your feelings.
- It helps you understand and explain where you are in your relationship.
- It empowers you to become the best you can be for yourself and your partner.

To proceed with your Relationship Reality Check, sign the Partner's Starting Agreement on the next page. If you are reading this book alone, your partner's signature is not necessary for you to check and understand where you are in your relationship. However, if you are reading this book with your partner and both of you want a healthy, mutually supportive relationship, then both partners can sign it now.

PARTNER'S STARTING AGREEMENT

BILL OF RELATIONSHIP RIGHTS

We, the undersigned, agree: Both partners in this relationship are individual human beings and deserve to be treated that way. We both respect each other's human qualities and human rights. The following are the Relationship Rights that I agree to honor for my partner and myself:

Partner's Acceptance:

Signature _____   **Date** _____

Signature _____   **Date** _____

(Purchase of this book entitles the buyer to reproduce this contract for personal use or use with a marriage & family counselor)

THE BILL OF RELATIONSHIP RIGHTS

YOUR RELATIONSHIP GUIDE

A list of the elements found in mutually supportive relationships

Use this list as a guide to understand your own relationship and/or to communicate your feelings about the presence or absence of these elements in your relationship.

Your Personal Rights: Green Rights
GO with your personal resources

___ Achievements
___ Balance
___ Creativity and Ideas
___ Dignity
___ Dreams and Goals
___ Energy
___ Family

___ Feelings
___ Financial Discretion
___ Friends
___ Health
___ Intelligence
___ Motivations
___ Opinions and Tastes

___ Reality
___ Safe Haven
___ Space
___ Spirituality
___ Talents and Career
___ Time

Your Benefit Rights: Yellow Rights
CAUTION if you aren't receiving relationship benefits

___ Acceptance
___ Acknowledgement
___ Apologies
___ Appreciation
___ Atmosphere
___ Caring
___ Cherishing
___ Commitment
___ Communication
___ Companionship
___ Compromise
___ Conflict Rsesolution

___ Emotional Support
___ Empathy
___ Encouragement
___ Equality
___ Flexibility
___ Forgiveness
___ Friendship
___ Honesty
___ Intimacy
___ Kindness
___ Love
___ Mutuality

___ Optimism
___ Reliability
___ Respect
___ Responsibility Sharing
___ Sense of Humor
___ Sensitivity
___ Sharing
___ Trust
___ Understanding
___ Warmth

Your Safety Rights: Red Rights
STOP tolerating harmful behaviors; you should feel safe in your relationship

___ Safe from Accusation and Blame
___ Safe from Anger
___ Safe from Being Assigned Status
___ Safe from Black-and-White Thinking
___ Safe from Button-Pushing and Brainwashing
___ Safe from Constant Complaining
___ Safe from Control

___ Safe from Denial and Avoidance
___ Safe from Discounting and Diverting
___ Safe from Entitlement
___ Safe from Humiliation
___ Safe from Hurtful Physical or Sexual Behaviors
___ Safe from Indifference
___ Safe from Judgment and Criticism

___ Safe from being Ordered
___ Safe from being a Possession
___ Safe from Responsibility for Another's Happiness
___ Safe from Rewriting History
___ Safe from Shame and Punishment
___ Safe from Threats
___ Safe from Tone of Voice

Chapter Nine

DO A RELATIONSHIP REALITY CHECK

Your Relationship Isn't Perfect, but How Good or Bad Is It?

How good or bad is your relationship? Some of your problems might be small, but others seem huge. On the other hand, your relationship has good qualities, too. But how good do they have to be to outweigh the bad? Are you making mountains out of molehills, or are you truly not well off? Help! These are the same questions we asked ourselves when we tried to evaluate our relationships.

To evaluate a relationship, one friend suggested listing all the good points in one column, listing all the bad points in another, and then comparing the two. But this process was woefully inadequate because we also needed some way to measure the strength or severity of each of the points. How good was good and how bad was bad? Another friend suggested weighing the relationship on a scale from zero to ten, but that was misleading because the answers could only be positive. Relationships not only support and enhance us as individuals, they also unfortunately can be hurtful and destructive. We needed to visualize where our relationships were taking us.

[129]

On our journey down the Relationship Road, we needed a map with guidelines and checkpoints but we also needed a Relationship Scale to measure how far we were from our goal or destination. Every map has a scale to show the relative distance between points on the map, such as one inch equals one hundred miles. We also needed a relative way to measure how much our relationships were enhancing or hurting us as individuals. Were we moving closer to our goal or further away? The Relationship Scale would give us the means to measure how we felt about our Relationship Rights. Were our partners supporting and encouraging us? Or were they more concerned about controlling us? Were our relationships a benefit or detriment? Were we being enhanced or hurt? And most of all, the scale would help us determine "How much we were being enhanced" and "How much we were being hurt." To do a Relationship Reality Check, we used the scale to measure how we feel about each of our rights. How much were our relationship rights supported or denied? How far were our relationships taking us in one direction or the other?

Again, we go back to the fairy-tale relationship we dreamt about.
Here are the Charming Prince and Fair Princess riding off to *Happily-Ever-After*. They're trotting along when they come to some rocks and boulders in the road. Does it shake them loose and throw them off, or do they hold on to each other for comfort and stability? How do they make it over the hills and through the valleys? Do they build bridges and clear paths together? Do these roadblocks strengthen them as a couple or make them fall apart? Are they able to get over the roadblocks and continue on toward *Happily-Ever-After*, or are they heading in another direction? How do they know where they are?

If you and your partner are lost, what do you do? You look to find street signs, signals, or indications that you're going in the right direction and then figure out the distance you need to travel. It's good to recognize you're lost or getting off the path as soon as possible so that you don't get too far out of the way and it's not too hard to correct your course and make up for lost time.

For example, will you know where you are in your relationship if these things happen...

a) You see something you passed when you were five or ten years younger. You tap your partner gently and say, "Wait a minute, I'm going backward. I've been here before." You might find yourself in *NeverNeverLand*, where people never grow up or develop, just like Peter Pan.
You're getting older, but you're not able to grow as a person. Your relationship has taken you backward.

b) Along the trip your partner says, "Move aside; I'm steering this stallion."

You ask, "But don't I have some say in where we are going?"

You lose control of your direction in life and get lost along the way.

c) Your horse's hoofs get tangled in the reins, and you get stuck in one place.

This is neither good nor bad, just stuck.

d) You and your partner take turns with the reins of the stallion so that each helps the other in steering the course of the relationship.

Neither partner gets fatigued, and neither controls the other. You'll reach Happily-Ever-After with plenty of energy left.

e) Your relationship is galloping forward as you are growing, but you don't have time to share. Maybe you need to slow down a bit and walk through a beautiful flower garden—the flowers might like to see you.

You may want to slow down and enjoy yourselves, the scenery, and life on your way.

f) Your relationship is alternately walking and trotting forward at a slow but steady pace.

You can see Happily-Ever-After on the horizon.

So, where are you on the Relationship Road? Is most of it smooth? Is it taking you forward or backward? Can you see *Happily-Ever-After* off in the distance? Are you getter closer? You don't have to go so fast that you don't have time to appreciate the little things. Or is your relationship actually taking you backward? When you go backward, do you go so far back and miss so many opportunities that any forward motion can't make up for your losses? The sooner you recognize where your relationship is taking you as a person, the sooner you will be able to correct your course. If you haven't gotten too far off the road, the course correction might be quite small but meaningful. The longer you let it stay off course or the farther you let it go in the wrong direction, the harder it is to fix.

Each of the rights listed in the Relationship Guide are checkpoints on the way to *Happily-Ever-After*. We developed a Relationship Scale to measure where you are with each of your rights at the checkpoints in your relationship. Are you going forward, backward, or standing still? Are your rights being developed, denied, or are they neutral? Not every right has the same importance to each individual. That's what makes us unique. The Relationship Scale is therefore unique for each individual. It is based on how you feel; there are no right or wrong answers; no one can tell you how to fill it out.

THE RELATIONSHIP SCALE

The Relationship Scale is a self-measuring system of how good you feel about yourself as a person in your relationship.

- It is completely gender-neutral.
- The answers are based strictly on how each person feels.
- No one dictates how you should answer—you need to be honest with yourself.

The Relationship Scale

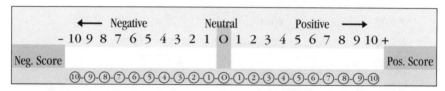

The Relationship Scale is designed to give you an actual picture of your feelings about your relationship, both positive and negative. You can easily see which way the scale is tipping. It is very visual. Is it tipping positively or negatively? It will also show you where you feel you are in your relationship as an individual. As you can see from the diagram above, the scale goes from "0," which is neutral, up to "+10," which is the most positive (indicating that your rights are positively supported/encouraged), and down to "-10," which is the most negative (showing that your rights are being controlled, denied, or not respected). The Relationship Scale is not limited to a positive range because at times you might truly feel that you are "in the hole" or your relationship is taking you backward.

Each of your Relationship Rights can fall anywhere on the scale. As you go through each of your rights listed in the Green, Yellow, and Red categories, mark them on the Relationship Scale according to how you feel they are supported or denied by your partner.

Scoring all of your Relationship Rights on the Relationship Scale is an eye-opening experience because most of us tend to gloss over some parts of our relationships. Often we don't even know all the questions we should ask ourselves because we might be so concerned about keeping the relationship together and being supportive of our partner that we aren't even aware of our rights. On the other hand, our partners are often unaware of how they might actually be hurting us because of their prior expectations, cultural backgrounds, environments, or ignorance. If they realized and saw how their actions were hurting us, they might change.

When you do your Relationship Reality Check using the Relationship Scale as your basis for scoring, you will be able to focus on the components of your relationship and how your partner makes you feel. Remember, only you know how you feel.

After completing your Relationship Reality Check, you might choose to write in a separate notebook and use our suggested journaling topics in Chapter Thirteen, "The Write Thing." Writing will help give you further insight into your rights, as well as help you find some positive ways your partner can be more supportive. You'll also find suggestions for sharing your Relationship Reality Check with your partner and for working with a relationship therapist. The Resources and Referrals section in Appendix A might also be helpful if you or your family need special help.

HOW DO YOU FEEL IN YOUR RELATIONSHIP?

Now let's discover how you feel about your relationship. Remember that your Relationship Reality Check is based on the Partners' Starting Agreement that "Both partners in a relationship are individual human beings who deserve to be treated that way."

Using the scoring described for the Relationship Scale, rank each of your Relationship Rights for how positively or negatively you feel your partner supports or denies them for you as an individual human being. Does your partner encourage and support you and your rights? Or does your partner hold you back, try to control you, or hurt you either emotionally or physically? Remember, your score can be anywhere on the scale between -10 up to +10.

Decide how you feel about each of the rights in your relationship as they are listed, put an "x" through the circle representing your score, and then write the score in either the positive or negative column next to that right. An example follows for the Green Right of Achievements:

SAMPLE POSITIVE SCORE

If you feel your partner regularly supports and encourages your achievements and often makes you feel good about them, then mark the Relationship Scale with a highly positive number like #8.

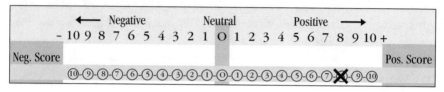

SAMPLE NEUTRAL SCORE

If you feel your partner neither supports nor denies, disrespects, or puts down your achievements, then mark a number in the neutral zone around 0, plus or minus 3.

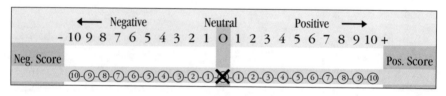

SAMPLE NEGATIVE SCORE

If you feel your partner sometimes, although not all the time, puts you down and refuses to acknowledge or respect you and your accomplishments, mark the Relationship Scale with a negative number, perhaps a -3 to -5. If it's more severe, then mark a more negative number.

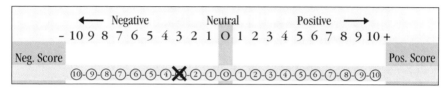

If you have questions about the meaning of a right or are unsure about how you feel, refer back to the definitions of each of your rights, which are listed alphabetically in Chapters Five, Six, and Seven. Or you can go to www.relationshiprights.com for even more comprehensive descriptions of rights listing different aspects of each right and expanded descriptions of how each right can make you feel when it is supported or denied.

YOUR GREEN RIGHTS REALITY CHECK

1. Score each of your Green Rights listed on the opposite page from -10 to +10, based on how strongly you feel your partner supports or denies it in your relationship.

    Put an "X" or darken the appropriate circle on the line for each Green Right listed. Then write the actual score to the right of the line if it is positive or 0 and to the left of the line if the score is negative.

If you have questions about the meaning of any of the rights listed, refer to its definition in Chapter Five.

You might find the following questions helpful, where applicable, as you score each of your Green Rights:
*   Is this personal right under my control, or does my partner dictate it?
*   Do I recognize this personal right as a reflection of my identity or of my partner's?
*   Am I free to develop and use this personal right to the fullest extent, or has my partner taken away my ability to develop or appreciate it?
*   Does my partner "use up" this personal right to the extent that there is nothing left for me to use for myself?
*   Is this personal right alive and well, or is it going downhill or even dead?
*   Does my partner support and encourage me to use this personal right so that I feel good as an individual?
*   Am I accomplishing my goals and will I reach my full potential and enjoyment by using this personal right?
*   Do I feel encouraged to be independent from my partner in using this personal right?

After you have finished filling out your Green Rights Relationship Scale, take a look at the page. How do your Green Rights look?
*   Do you feel your personal qualities are being developed, shared, and encouraged by your partner?
*   Do you feel overall good about where you are going as a person in the relationship?
*   Do you feel that you are able to develop your own identity as a separate person? Or does it look like you are being controlled by your partner?
*   Are you moving forward or backwards as an individual in your relationship? How far forward or backward does it look like you are going?
*   Which rights, if any, need to be worked on the most?

GREEN RIGHTS SCALE

Ask yourself the following question regarding each of your Green Rights/ Personal Rights listed below and mark how strongly positive or negative your partner supports it. **Does my partner accept, support or encourage my own...**

	Neg. Score	← Negative Neutral Positive → - 10 9 8 7 6 5 4 3 2 1 0 1 2 3 4 5 6 7 8 9 10 +	Pos. Score
Achievements		⑩-⑨-⑧-⑦-⑥-⑤-④-③-②-①-⓪-①-②-③-④-⑤-⑥-⑦-⑧-⑨-⑩	
Balance		⑩-⑨-⑧-⑦-⑥-⑤-④-③-②-①-⓪-①-②-③-④-⑤-⑥-⑦-⑧-⑨-⑩	
Creativity		⑩-⑨-⑧-⑦-⑥-⑤-④-③-②-①-⓪-①-②-③-④-⑤-⑥-⑦-⑧-⑨-⑩	
Dignity		⑩-⑨-⑧-⑦-⑥-⑤-④-③-②-①-⓪-①-②-③-④-⑤-⑥-⑦-⑧-⑨-⑩	
Dreams/Goals		⑩-⑨-⑧-⑦-⑥-⑤-④-③-②-①-⓪-①-②-③-④-⑤-⑥-⑦-⑧-⑨-⑩	
Energy		⑩-⑨-⑧-⑦-⑥-⑤-④-③-②-①-⓪-①-②-③-④-⑤-⑥-⑦-⑧-⑨-⑩	
Family		⑩-⑨-⑧-⑦-⑥-⑤-④-③-②-①-⓪-①-②-③-④-⑤-⑥-⑦-⑧-⑨-⑩	
Feelings		⑩-⑨-⑧-⑦-⑥-⑤-④-③-②-①-⓪-①-②-③-④-⑤-⑥-⑦-⑧-⑨-⑩	
Financial Discretion		⑩-⑨-⑧-⑦-⑥-⑤-④-③-②-①-⓪-①-②-③-④-⑤-⑥-⑦-⑧-⑨-⑩	
Friends		⑩-⑨-⑧-⑦-⑥-⑤-④-③-②-①-⓪-①-②-③-④-⑤-⑥-⑦-⑧-⑨-⑩	
Health		⑩-⑨-⑧-⑦-⑥-⑤-④-③-②-①-⓪-①-②-③-④-⑤-⑥-⑦-⑧-⑨-⑩	
Intelligence		⑩-⑨-⑧-⑦-⑥-⑤-④-③-②-①-⓪-①-②-③-④-⑤-⑥-⑦-⑧-⑨-⑩	
Motivations		⑩-⑨-⑧-⑦-⑥-⑤-④-③-②-①-⓪-①-②-③-④-⑤-⑥-⑦-⑧-⑨-⑩	
Opinions/Taste		⑩-⑨-⑧-⑦-⑥-⑤-④-③-②-①-⓪-①-②-③-④-⑤-⑥-⑦-⑧-⑨-⑩	
Reality		⑩-⑨-⑧-⑦-⑥-⑤-④-③-②-①-⓪-①-②-③-④-⑤-⑥-⑦-⑧-⑨-⑩	
Safe Haven		⑩-⑨-⑧-⑦-⑥-⑤-④-③-②-①-⓪-①-②-③-④-⑤-⑥-⑦-⑧-⑨-⑩	
Space		⑩-⑨-⑧-⑦-⑥-⑤-④-③-②-①-⓪-①-②-③-④-⑤-⑥-⑦-⑧-⑨-⑩	
Spirituality		⑩-⑨-⑧-⑦-⑥-⑤-④-③-②-①-⓪-①-②-③-④-⑤-⑥-⑦-⑧-⑨-⑩	
Talents/Career		⑩-⑨-⑧-⑦-⑥-⑤-④-③-②-①-⓪-①-②-③-④-⑤-⑥-⑦-⑧-⑨-⑩	
Time		⑩-⑨-⑧-⑦-⑥-⑤-④-③-②-①-⓪-①-②-③-④-⑤-⑥-⑦-⑧-⑨-⑩	
TOTALS	Negative		Positive

YOUR YELLOW RIGHTS REALITY CHECK

1. Score each of your Yellow Rights listed on the opposite page from -10 to +10, based on how strongly you feel your partner supports or denies benefits for you in the relationship.

    Put an "X" or darken the appropriate circle on the line for each Yellow Right listed. Then write the actual score to the right of the line if it is positive or 0 and to the left of the line if the score is negative.

If you have questions about the meaning of any of the rights listed, refer to its definition in Chapter Six.

You might find the following questions helpful as you score each of your Yellow Rights:
- Does my partner support me with this feeling or behavior?
- Is the feeling evident in my partner's actions or is it only lip service?
- How often does my partner give me these benefits?
- Do I enhance my partner's growth by showing this feeling or behavior?
- Do my partner's behaviors make me feel special and enhanced as an individual?
- How strongly does my partner support or deny each of my Yellow Rights?

After you have finished filling out your Yellow Rights Relationship Scale, take a look at the page. How do your Yellow Rights look?
- Are you getting the benefits of being in your relationship?
- Does your relationship look comfortable, intimate, and warm?
- Is your relationship encouraging and supportive?
- Are you sharing and close?
- Is there laugher and fun?
- How about mutuality?
- Does it look like you could just as well be roommates?
- What areas, if any, would you like to see improved?

YELLOW RIGHTS SCALE

Ask yourself this question regarding each of your Yellow Right/Relationship Rights listed below and mark how strongly positive or negative your partner supports it. **Does my partner give me...**

← Negative   Neutral   Positive →

-10 9 8 7 6 5 4 3 2 1 0 1 2 3 4 5 6 7 8 9 10 +

	Neg. Score	Scale	Pos. Score
Acceptance		(10)-(9)-(8)-(7)-(6)-(5)-(4)-(3)-(2)-(1)-(0)-(1)-(2)-(3)-(4)-(5)-(6)-(7)-(8)-(9)-(10)	
Acknowledgement		(10)-(9)-(8)-(7)-(6)-(5)-(4)-(3)-(2)-(1)-(0)-(1)-(2)-(3)-(4)-(5)-(6)-(7)-(8)-(9)-(10)	
Apologies		(10)-(9)-(8)-(7)-(6)-(5)-(4)-(3)-(2)-(1)-(0)-(1)-(2)-(3)-(4)-(5)-(6)-(7)-(8)-(9)-(10)	
Appreciation		(10)-(9)-(8)-(7)-(6)-(5)-(4)-(3)-(2)-(1)-(0)-(1)-(2)-(3)-(4)-(5)-(6)-(7)-(8)-(9)-(10)	
Atmosphere		(10)-(9)-(8)-(7)-(6)-(5)-(4)-(3)-(2)-(1)-(0)-(1)-(2)-(3)-(4)-(5)-(6)-(7)-(8)-(9)-(10)	
Caring		(10)-(9)-(8)-(7)-(6)-(5)-(4)-(3)-(2)-(1)-(0)-(1)-(2)-(3)-(4)-(5)-(6)-(7)-(8)-(9)-(10)	
Cherishing		(10)-(9)-(8)-(7)-(6)-(5)-(4)-(3)-(2)-(1)-(0)-(1)-(2)-(3)-(4)-(5)-(6)-(7)-(8)-(9)-(10)	
Commitment		(10)-(9)-(8)-(7)-(6)-(5)-(4)-(3)-(2)-(1)-(0)-(1)-(2)-(3)-(4)-(5)-(6)-(7)-(8)-(9)-(10)	
Communication		(10)-(9)-(8)-(7)-(6)-(5)-(4)-(3)-(2)-(1)-(0)-(1)-(2)-(3)-(4)-(5)-(6)-(7)-(8)-(9)-(10)	
Companionship		(10)-(9)-(8)-(7)-(6)-(5)-(4)-(3)-(2)-(1)-(0)-(1)-(2)-(3)-(4)-(5)-(6)-(7)-(8)-(9)-(10)	
Compromise		(10)-(9)-(8)-(7)-(6)-(5)-(4)-(3)-(2)-(1)-(0)-(1)-(2)-(3)-(4)-(5)-(6)-(7)-(8)-(9)-(10)	
Conflict Resolution		(10)-(9)-(8)-(7)-(6)-(5)-(4)-(3)-(2)-(1)-(0)-(1)-(2)-(3)-(4)-(5)-(6)-(7)-(8)-(9)-(10)	
Emotional Support		(10)-(9)-(8)-(7)-(6)-(5)-(4)-(3)-(2)-(1)-(0)-(1)-(2)-(3)-(4)-(5)-(6)-(7)-(8)-(9)-(10)	
Empathy		(10)-(9)-(8)-(7)-(6)-(5)-(4)-(3)-(2)-(1)-(0)-(1)-(2)-(3)-(4)-(5)-(6)-(7)-(8)-(9)-(10)	
Encouragement		(10)-(9)-(8)-(7)-(6)-(5)-(4)-(3)-(2)-(1)-(0)-(1)-(2)-(3)-(4)-(5)-(6)-(7)-(8)-(9)-(10)	
Equality		(10)-(9)-(8)-(7)-(6)-(5)-(4)-(3)-(2)-(1)-(0)-(1)-(2)-(3)-(4)-(5)-(6)-(7)-(8)-(9)-(10)	
Flexibility		(10)-(9)-(8)-(7)-(6)-(5)-(4)-(3)-(2)-(1)-(0)-(1)-(2)-(3)-(4)-(5)-(6)-(7)-(8)-(9)-(10)	
Forgiveness		(10)-(9)-(8)-(7)-(6)-(5)-(4)-(3)-(2)-(1)-(0)-(1)-(2)-(3)-(4)-(5)-(6)-(7)-(8)-(9)-(10)	
Friendship		(10)-(9)-(8)-(7)-(6)-(5)-(4)-(3)-(2)-(1)-(0)-(1)-(2)-(3)-(4)-(5)-(6)-(7)-(8)-(9)-(10)	
Honesty		(10)-(9)-(8)-(7)-(6)-(5)-(4)-(3)-(2)-(1)-(0)-(1)-(2)-(3)-(4)-(5)-(6)-(7)-(8)-(9)-(10)	
Intimacy		(10)-(9)-(8)-(7)-(6)-(5)-(4)-(3)-(2)-(1)-(0)-(1)-(2)-(3)-(4)-(5)-(6)-(7)-(8)-(9)-(10)	
Kindness		(10)-(9)-(8)-(7)-(6)-(5)-(4)-(3)-(2)-(1)-(0)-(1)-(2)-(3)-(4)-(5)-(6)-(7)-(8)-(9)-(10)	
Love		(10)-(9)-(8)-(7)-(6)-(5)-(4)-(3)-(2)-(1)-(0)-(1)-(2)-(3)-(4)-(5)-(6)-(7)-(8)-(9)-(10)	
Mutuality		(10)-(9)-(8)-(7)-(6)-(5)-(4)-(3)-(2)-(1)-(0)-(1)-(2)-(3)-(4)-(5)-(6)-(7)-(8)-(9)-(10)	
Optimism		(10)-(9)-(8)-(7)-(6)-(5)-(4)-(3)-(2)-(1)-(0)-(1)-(2)-(3)-(4)-(5)-(6)-(7)-(8)-(9)-(10)	
Reliability		(10)-(9)-(8)-(7)-(6)-(5)-(4)-(3)-(2)-(1)-(0)-(1)-(2)-(3)-(4)-(5)-(6)-(7)-(8)-(9)-(10)	
Respect		(10)-(9)-(8)-(7)-(6)-(5)-(4)-(3)-(2)-(1)-(0)-(1)-(2)-(3)-(4)-(5)-(6)-(7)-(8)-(9)-(10)	
Responsibility Sharing		(10)-(9)-(8)-(7)-(6)-(5)-(4)-(3)-(2)-(1)-(0)-(1)-(2)-(3)-(4)-(5)-(6)-(7)-(8)-(9)-(10)	
Sense of Humor		(10)-(9)-(8)-(7)-(6)-(5)-(4)-(3)-(2)-(1)-(0)-(1)-(2)-(3)-(4)-(5)-(6)-(7)-(8)-(9)-(10)	
Sensitivity		(10)-(9)-(8)-(7)-(6)-(5)-(4)-(3)-(2)-(1)-(0)-(1)-(2)-(3)-(4)-(5)-(6)-(7)-(8)-(9)-(10)	
Sharing		(10)-(9)-(8)-(7)-(6)-(5)-(4)-(3)-(2)-(1)-(0)-(1)-(2)-(3)-(4)-(5)-(6)-(7)-(8)-(9)-(10)	
Trust		(10)-(9)-(8)-(7)-(6)-(5)-(4)-(3)-(2)-(1)-(0)-(1)-(2)-(3)-(4)-(5)-(6)-(7)-(8)-(9)-(10)	
Understanding		(10)-(9)-(8)-(7)-(6)-(5)-(4)-(3)-(2)-(1)-(0)-(1)-(2)-(3)-(4)-(5)-(6)-(7)-(8)-(9)-(10)	
Warmth		(10)-(9)-(8)-(7)-(6)-(5)-(4)-(3)-(2)-(1)-(0)-(1)-(2)-(3)-(4)-(5)-(6)-(7)-(8)-(9)-(10)	
TOTALS	Negative		Positive

YOUR RED RIGHTS REALITY CHECK

1. Score each of your Red Rights listed on the opposite page from -10 to +10, based on how strongly you feel your partner supports or denies your right to be safe from each hurtful behavior.

   Put an "X" or darken the appropriate circle on the line for each Red Right listed. Then write the actual score to the right of the line if it is positive or 0 and to the left of the line if the score is negative.

If you have questions about the meaning of any of the rights listed, refer to its definition in Chapter Seven.

You might find the following questions helpful as you score each of your Red Rights:
- Does this behavior exist in my relationship?
- Does this behavior happen frequently?
- Am I afraid of my partner because of this behavior?
- Do I walk on eggshells around my partner for fear the behavior will erupt at any time?
- Do I feel safe with my partner both emotionally and physically?
- Does this behavior provide a positive or negative living environment for me and my family?
- Does my partner twist things around to the point that I question my reality and feelings?
- Does my partner exhibit these hurtful behaviors only when with the family or in the privacy of our home and then look like a saint in public?
- Does my partner make me feel stupid or like there is something wrong with me when I point out this hurtful behavior in our relationship?

After you have finished filling out your Red Rights Relationship Scale, take a look at it. How do your Red Rights look?
- Are you being respected or hurt?
- If you are being respected, you probably have very few Red Right negatives. If any, what are they?
- If you are not being respected, there may be many areas where your Red Rights are violated. What are they?
- If you are being hurt, do you think your partner realizes the behaviors are harmful? Do you think your partner cares?
- Does this page show you whether you are living in a positive or a negative environment?

RED RIGHTS SCALE

Ask yourself this question regarding each of your Red Right/Freedom Rights listed below and mark how strongly positive or negative your partner support: it. **In my relationship with my partner, am I free from...**

	← Negative	Neutral	Positive →	
	− 10 9 8 7 6 5 4 3 2 1	0	1 2 3 4 5 6 7 8 9 10 +	
	Neg. Score			Pos. Score
Accusation & Blame	⑩-⑨-⑧-⑦-⑥-⑤-④-③-②-①	-⓪-	①-②-③-④-⑤-⑥-⑦-⑧-⑨-⑩	
Anger	⑩-⑨-⑧-⑦-⑥-⑤-④-③-②-①	-⓪-	①-②-③-④-⑤-⑥-⑦-⑧-⑨-⑩	
Assigned Status	⑩-⑨-⑧-⑦-⑥-⑤-④-③-②-①	-⓪-	①-②-③-④-⑤-⑥-⑦-⑧-⑨-⑩	
Black/White Thinking	⑩-⑨-⑧-⑦-⑥-⑤-④-③-②-①	-⓪-	①-②-③-④-⑤-⑥-⑦-⑧-⑨-⑩	
Button Push & Brainwash	⑩-⑨-⑧-⑦-⑥-⑤-④-③-②-①	-⓪-	①-②-③-④-⑤-⑥-⑦-⑧-⑨-⑩	
Constant Complaining	⑩-⑨-⑧-⑦-⑥-⑤-④-③-②-①	-⓪-	①-②-③-④-⑤-⑥-⑦-⑧-⑨-⑩	
Control	⑩-⑨-⑧-⑦-⑥-⑤-④-③-②-①	-⓪-	①-②-③-④-⑤-⑥-⑦-⑧-⑨-⑩	
Denial & Avoidance	⑩-⑨-⑧-⑦-⑥-⑤-④-③-②-①	-⓪-	①-②-③-④-⑤-⑥-⑦-⑧-⑨-⑩	
Discounting & Diverting	⑩-⑨-⑧-⑦-⑥-⑤-④-③-②-①	-⓪-	①-②-③-④-⑤-⑥-⑦-⑧-⑨-⑩	
Entitlement	⑩-⑨-⑧-⑦-⑥-⑤-④-③-②-①	-⓪-	①-②-③-④-⑤-⑥-⑦-⑧-⑨-⑩	
Humiliation	⑩-⑨-⑧-⑦-⑥-⑤-④-③-②-①	-⓪-	①-②-③-④-⑤-⑥-⑦-⑧-⑨-⑩	
Hurtful-Physical & Sex	⑩-⑨-⑧-⑦-⑥-⑤-④-③-②-①	-⓪-	①-②-③-④-⑤-⑥-⑦-⑧-⑨-⑩	
Indifference	⑩-⑨-⑧-⑦-⑥-⑤-④-③-②-①	-⓪-	①-②-③-④-⑤-⑥-⑦-⑧-⑨-⑩	
Judgment & Criticism	⑩-⑨-⑧-⑦-⑥-⑤-④-③-②-①	-⓪-	①-②-③-④-⑤-⑥-⑦-⑧-⑨-⑩	
Being Ordered	⑩-⑨-⑧-⑦-⑥-⑤-④-③-②-①	-⓪-	①-②-③-④-⑤-⑥-⑦-⑧-⑨-⑩	
Being a Possession	⑩-⑨-⑧-⑦-⑥-⑤-④-③-②-①	-⓪-	①-②-③-④-⑤-⑥-⑦-⑧-⑨-⑩	
Respons. for Happiness	⑩-⑨-⑧-⑦-⑥-⑤-④-③-②-①	-⓪-	①-②-③-④-⑤-⑥-⑦-⑧-⑨-⑩	
Rewriting History	⑩-⑨-⑧-⑦-⑥-⑤-④-③-②-①	-⓪-	①-②-③-④-⑤-⑥-⑦-⑧-⑨-⑩	
Shame & Punishment	⑩-⑨-⑧-⑦-⑥-⑤-④-③-②-①	-⓪-	①-②-③-④-⑤-⑥-⑦-⑧-⑨-⑩	
Threats	⑩-⑨-⑧-⑦-⑥-⑤-④-③-②-①	-⓪-	①-②-③-④-⑤-⑥-⑦-⑧-⑨-⑩	
Tone of Voice	⑩-⑨-⑧-⑦-⑥-⑤-④-③-②-①	-⓪-	①-②-③-④-⑤-⑥-⑦-⑧-⑨-⑩	
TOTALS	Negative		Positive	

SUMMARIZE YOUR SCORES

(Skip this section if you do not want to do the math and go directly to Chapter Ten)

For many people, seeing the scoring of their rights on the Relationship Scale gives them a full visual picture of their relationship. If the visual picture of your Relationship Rights Scale is enough, you can skip to Chapter Ten. However, if you would like to average your scores, you can do so by following the directions below.

Go back to your scoring pages for each of the Green, Yellow, and Red Rights and with a calculator total the negative columns and the positive columns of scores you marked for each. Fill in the totals for each column on the appropriate lines marked "Negative" and "Positive."

Then transfer those totals to the respective Negative and Positive Totals lines and follow the directions to get your Green, Yellow, and Red Rights average scores.

SAMPLE SCORING FOR YOUR GREEN RIGHTS

A. **If your positive total is larger than your negative total (example: negative total -20 and positive total 110), your answer will look like this:**

1. Transfer both your negative and positive score column totals from the Green Rights Scale page and write the totals on the "total lines" below. Make sure to put a negative in front of the negative total.

   Negative Column Total: ___-20___   Positive Column Total: ___110___

2. Fill in the lines below with the negative and positive totals from #1 above. Then, with your calculator, add your negative total (making sure to precede your negative total with the negative sign) to your positive total and write the new total below. Note that it is a positive number.

   Negative Column Total + Positive Column Total = Total Score

   ___-20___   +   ___110___   =   ___90___

3. Determine your final Green Rights score by dividing the Total Score above by 20.

   Total Green Score: ___+90___ ÷ 20 = Green Rights Average Support ___+4.5___

OR

B. **If your negative total is larger than your positive total (example: negative total -163 and positive total 118), your answer will look like this:**

1. Transfer both your negative and positive score column totals from the Green Relationship Scale page and write the totals on the "total lines" below. Make sure to put a negative sign in front of the negative total.

   Negative Column Total: __-163__   Positive Column Total: __+118__

2. Fill in the lines below with the negative and positive totals from #1 above. Then, with your calculator, add your negative total (making sure to precede your negative total with the negative sign) to your positive total and write the new total below. Note that it is a negative number.

   Negative Column Total + Positive Column Total = Total Score

   __-163__   +   __118__   =   __-45__

3. Determine your final Green Rights score by dividing the Total Score above by 20.

   Total Green Score: __-45__ ÷ 20 = Green Rights Average Support __-2.5__

GREEN RIGHTS AVERAGE SUPPORT

1. Transfer both your negative and positive score column totals from the Green Rights Scale page and write the totals on the Negative and Positive Column Total lines below.

   Negative Column Total: _____   Positive Column Total: _____

2. Fill in the lines below with the negative and positive totals from #1 above. Then, with your calculator, add your Negative Column Total (making sure to precede your negative total with the negative sign) to your Positive Column Total and write the new total under Total Score.

   Negative Column Total + Positive Column Total = Total Score

   _____   +   _____   =   _____

   (indicate whether Total Score is positive or negative)

3. Determine your final Green Rights Average Support by dividing the Total Score above by 20.

Total Score from above: _____ ÷ 20 = Final Green Rights Average Support _____

(indicate whether Final Average Score is positive or negative)

[143]

YELLOW RIGHTS AVERAGE SUPPORT

1. Transfer both your negative and positive score column totals from the Yellow Rights Scale page and write the totals on the Negative and Positive Column Total lines below.

    Negative Column Total: _____   Positive Column Total: _____

2. Fill in the lines below with the negative and positive totals from #1 above. Then, with your calculator, add your Negative Column Total (making sure to precede your negative total with the negative sign) to your Positive Column Total and write the new total to the right below under Total Score.

    Negative Column Total + Positive Column Total = Total Score

    _____   +   _____   =   _____

    (indicate whether Total Score is positive or negative)

3. Determine your Yellow Rights Average Support by dividing the Total Score above by 34.

Total Score from above: _____ ÷ 34 = Final Yellow Rights Average Support _____
(indicate whether Final Average Score is positive or negative)

RED RIGHTS AVERAGE SUPPORT

1. Transfer both your negative and positive score column totals from the Red Rights Scale page and write the totals on the Negative and Positive Column Total lines below.

    Negative Column Total: _____   Positive Column Total: _____

2. Fill in the lines below with the negative and positive totals from #1 above. Then, with your calculator, add your Negative Column Total (making sure to precede your negative total with the minus sign) to your Positive Column Total and write the new total under Total Score.

    Negative Column Total + Positive Column Total = Total Score

    _____   +   _____   =   _____

    (indicate whether Total Score is positive or negative)

3. With your calculator, determine your Red Rights Average Support by dividing the Total Score above by 21.

Total Score from above: _____ ÷ 21 = Final Red Rights Average Support _____
(indicate whether Final Average Score is positive or negative)

Chapter Ten

UNDERSTANDING THE RESULTS OF YOUR RELATIONSHIP REALITY CHECK

WHAT YOUR REALITY CHECK TELLS YOU ABOUT YOUR RELATIONSHIP

YOUR FINAL GREEN RIGHTS SCORE

Your final Green Rights score shows how your partner supports or denies your personal rights in your relationship. Are you allowed to be yourself and encouraged to develop as an individual? Or are you being controlled by someone else and being denied your personal expression, time, and development?

YOUR FINAL GREEN RIGHTS SCORE

When most of your Green Rights scores are positive, your partner encourages you to develop and reach your full potential as an individual.

Your relationship is supportive of you as a person. Your partner respects you and the relationship. Your partner encourages you and freely gives you support in your development as an individual human being. You can work toward filling your potential, and your partner's positive support makes it easier for you to do so. Certainly some areas

[145]

might be improved, but no relationship is perfect. You now know what these areas are and can work with your partner to improve them. Overall, you are benefiting from your partner's support and encouragement in this relationship. Recognize your partner for this, and offer thanks for the support. Make sure you are providing the same support.

When your Green Rights scores are close to zero, your partner accepts you as a separate individual.

If your score is close to zero, your relationship is neither encouraging nor discouraging your development. Your partner might not be encouraging you to develop yourself, but your partner seems to respect your individuality and isn't trying to hurt or control you. As far as developing your personal rights, you are on your own. You might want to take a look at your development as a person and decide whether you are happy with whom you are. Talk to your partner about how you are feeling and try to find ways he or she can be more encouraging and supportive.

When your Green Rights scores are negative, you might feel your partner doesn't allow you to be yourself in your relationship.

You should take a serious look at what your relationship is doing to you as an individual. Were you a separate and whole person before you became involved with your partner? Is your personal development stagnated by your relationship? Or have you actually lost ground? If you have gone backward in your personal development, you might want to consider whether you should stay in this relationship or whether you would be better off unattached. If you left, you might be more able to be yourself and develop to your full potential without someone denying you your personal rights. Your relationship might be detracting from you as an individual, and you could have difficulty reaching your full potential or controlling the balance in your life. Is someone else telling you what you should or shouldn't be or do? What changes need to be made in your relationship for you to be respected and to develop as an individual?

YOUR FINAL YELLOW RIGHTS SCORE

Your final Yellow Rights score shows whether you are getting the benefits you deserve from your relationship. Are you getting most of these benefits in your relationship? Or are you just sharing the title of "couple"?

When your Yellow Rights scores are positive, you are receiving the benefits of being in a relationship.

Your relationship is likely enhancing you as a person. You are feeling added warmth, trust, and intimacy with a special closeness and understanding. In difficult times, you know you can rely on your partner to be there to support you, soothe you, and show concern about how you feel. In good times, your joy doubles because you have someone to share it with. If you have problems, your partner is there to help. And when differences arise, you have little fear of confrontations because your differences are respected. Your relationship is based on give and take because your partner understands the importance of compromise and conflict resolution. Because no relationship is perfect, some areas could be improved. You know what these areas are and can work with your partner to improve them. Overall, you are benefiting from the added strength, warmth, honesty, and sharing in this relationship.

When your Yellow Rights scores are close to zero, you are probably receiving a sporadic mix of relationship benefits that are not consistent or strong enough to be positive and enhancing.

If your score is close to zero, your partner needs to exert more effort to make you feel special and show that he or she cares. Would you have scored your Yellow Rights any differently at the beginning of your relationship than now? If you would have, you might want to do an evaluation of how your score has changed over time. Has the importance of your relationship changed? Have you and your partner simply slipped into "ho-hum-drum"? Or were your expectations, goals, and beliefs unrealistic to start with? If there has been a change, why? Are you satisfied and content with the change? Understand that relationships change over time as they mature. The benefits may shift from being passionate to comfortable, or intense to moderate, but benefits are still important in order to continue validation of the relationship. If you aren't receiving benefits, you might want to share your scores with your partner to develop a new closeness and warmth in your relationship.

When your Yellow Rights scores are negative, you likely are not receiving enough benefits for being in a relationship.

You might want to think about the reasons you came into this relationship. As things now stand, your relationship is not enhancing you as an individual or adding to your quality of life. Your relationship might feel lopsided, and you might feel as if you are the only one giving to the partnership. You might want to consider whether you should stay in this relationship or whether you are better off alone and unattached. You might feel as though you are living with a roommate with the added complications of one-sided emotional entanglements and relationship responsibilities. If you do, what makes you feel this way? What changes need to be made to give you the benefits you deserve? Is your partner able to change? Is your partner willing to change?

YOUR FINAL RED RIGHTS SCORE

Your final Red Rights score shows whether you are free from harmful behaviors in your relationship or whether you fear being hurt by your partner either emotionally or physically. Red Rights are almost an "all or nothing" situation. If your partner respects you as a separate individual, your partner won't want to hurt you—he or she will violate very few, if any, of your Red Rights. However, if your partner doesn't respect you and doesn't care how he or she makes you feel, then how many rights are violated doesn't matter. The Red Right violations are an indication of disrespect.

Some partners are brought up with the belief that in order to be a successful partner, they must control you. They may use whatever means are necessary in order to exert and maintain their control, no matter how much it may hurt you. They defend their actions as righteous. They are not aware of the concept of Red Rights.

Many other partners are brought up with the belief that in order to be a successful partner, they must be obedient and submissive, no matter how much they are controlled, denied, or hurt. Because you were brought up this way doesn't mean that the behaviors aren't hurtful or that the control and hurt is acceptable.

When your Red Rights scores are positive, you are free from harmful behaviors in your relationship.

Your partner is respectful of you and your feelings and does not try to hurt or control you, either emotionally or physically. You can make mistakes without fear of punishment. Your partner accepts you without judgment or criticism as a separate and whole human being. You live in a positive environment and don't have to fear your partner in any way. When your partner does violate a Red Right, it's infrequent and is usually followed by a genuine apology.

When your Red Rights scores are close to zero, your partner occasionally makes a mistake but recognizes it and doesn't repeat it.

If your score is close to zero, your relationship is not completely free from harmful behaviors nor is it overrun with them. No one is perfect in a relationship, which is true for your partner as well as yourself. Your partner occasionally hurts you, but it's infrequent with no regular pattern and you're able to reconcile. The key is that the patterns don't repeat often and you don't live in fear. Keep the communication open and focus on how you and your partner might improve your relationship.

When your Red Rights scores are negative, you are not free from harmful behaviors in your relationship.

You need to stop your partner from hurting you, either physically or emotionally. You can now name your Red Right violations to your partner. You might be living in constant fear and might not know when and how your partner will erupt or attack next. Your partner will usually twist or justify behaviors and often blame you by telling you that you deserved or caused those behaviors. Sometimes you tolerate hurt because your partner will punish and hurt you more for defending yourself than for just tolerating the harmful behaviors. So you might allow the behaviors to continue because this is often less painful than resisting. You need to recognize what your partner is doing to you, especially emotionally. Are there particular issues or any of your Green Rights that trigger these behaviors? Is there a pattern of predictable scenarios for an outburst? Most of all, you need to recognize that your partner doesn't have a right to hurt you at all, at any time or for any reason. You've done nothing to deserve this, and you shouldn't tolerate harmful behaviors just to keep the relationship together. No one should have to live in a negative or fearful environment. You might want to strongly consider whether you want to stay in a harmful relationship, even though being alone or unattached might be tough. What changes need to be made to stop this hurt and prevent it from happening? How can you best do this?

WHERE ARE YOU?

Where are you in your relationship? Does it look as though you are moving toward *Happily-Ever-After*, have you stayed at neutral, or are you actually going backward? If you have calculated the final scores for your Green, Yellow, and Red Rights, darken the number that corresponds to each final score. Otherwise darken where it appears most of your Green, Yellow, and Red Rights are marked.

	Denied/Controlled		*Positively Supported/Encouraged*
	← Negative	Neutral	Positive →
	10 9 8 7 6 5 4 3 2 1	0	1 2 3 4 5 6 7 8 9 10
GREEN RIGHTS	⑩-⑨-⑧-⑦-⑥-⑤-④-③-②-①	-⓪-	①-②-③-④-⑤-⑥-⑦-⑧-⑨-⑩
YELLOW RIGHTS	⑩-⑨-⑧-⑦-⑥-⑤-④-③-②-①	-⓪-	①-②-③-④-⑤-⑥-⑦-⑧-⑨-⑩
RED RIGHTS	⑩-⑨-⑧-⑦-⑥-⑤-④-③-②-①	-⓪-	①-②-③-④-⑤-⑥-⑦-⑧-⑨-⑩

What does your relationship look like? Is it mostly positive, mostly negative, or a combination of positive and negative? In a relationship, you can be confused and even feel crazy at times, but this directional chart should help you clarify your feelings. The picture that you've created above can help show you whether your relationship is enhancing or hurting you as a human being. Where are you now?

If most of your scores are positive, congratulations! You have a wonderful relationship. Make sure that you are treating your partner the same way, with equal respect and support.

- Your relationship is enhancing your human qualities.
- Your partner not only accepts and respects you as an individual human being, he or she also feels a responsibility to support and encourage your development.
- You are able to expand and grow to your full potential with ease because you have a great supporter and cheerleader to give you added encouragement.
- Your relationship is a positive element in your life and it enhances you more than living alone would.
- You feel good about your relationship and have few problems or concerns.
- Losing your partner would be a sad event in your life.
- If there are a few areas in which your scores were not as high, you now know the areas to work on with your partner.
- Continue to communicate with your partner.
- Your partner is proud of you as a separate person, not as a possession.

Keep this relationship going; it should be a WIN/WIN for both you and your partner! Work to improve in the areas in which your scores are lowest. Keep reminding your partner how much you care.

If most of your scores are close to zero, your relationship is worthwhile, but with some focus on certain areas, it could be more enhancing.

- Your partner accepts and respects you as a human being and you are able to develop your full potential on your own.
- Your partner cares about you as a person, not just for what you give to the relationship.
- Your relationship is neither destructive nor encouraging.
- You might not have a lot of interaction with your partner, but that may be all right with you. You accept each other as human beings.
- You feel accepted in your relationship but don't necessarily feel that your partner is your cheerleader.
- If you want to develop your relationship further, you need to communicate and work with your partner on each Relationship Right that is important to you.
- If any Relationship Rights were strongly negative, you can work on developing

those with your partner. Any improvement can significantly increase the quality of your relationship and your total Relationship Scale score.

- If any Relationship Rights were strongly positive, thank your partner and express how good this makes you feel.
- Work on communicating your feelings about your human qualities to your partner, and you might find you'll get more support than you expect.
- Your relationship is satisfactory but can improve if you and your partner are willing to put in the time and effort to communicate and encourage each other.

You might want to work directly with your partner or with a counselor to improve various areas of your relationship. Refer to Chapter Thirteen, "The Write Thing." If you have difficulty discussing your feelings, try writing letters to each other first or order our Journaling Workbook. This will help you to organize your thoughts.

If most of your scores are negative, this relationship might be harmful to you as a person. You likely have some difficult decisions to make. Do you want to continue tolerating your relationship as it is? Do you want your relationship to improve? Do you want your relationship to end?

- Your partner might be holding you back from being yourself. You might even be unsure who "the real you" is; maybe you haven't been yourself for quite a while. You might also be afraid of being yourself for fear of being punished or reprimanded if you do not meet your partner's expectations. You might have to twist yourself into a pretzel in order to please your partner, and even then it isn't enough.
- Your relationship might be destructive to you as a human being. Your partner might be controlling you. Your partner might be denying your rights to your human qualities, and your relationship might in fact be destroying them. Your personal rights might have regressed from where they were before you got into your relationship.
- You might not be able to grow to your full potential in this relationship. Your partner might fight your individuality and your development.
- Your relationship might be a detrimental element in your life. You might catch yourself daydreaming about being single and the possibility that you would be much happier if you were able to be yourself without fear or criticism.
- Perhaps you have been feeling uneasy and concerned about your relationship but didn't always know how to explain or understand your feelings. Attempts to communicate your feelings to your partner might be met with defensiveness, argumentation, and outright anger rather than

with openness and concern for your feelings and well-being.

- You might not feel accepted or respected as an individual. Your partner might view you as a possession or see your purpose as a need-fulfiller. Your partner might need you to raise the family, take care of his or her personal needs, look good, provide sexual satisfaction, give social status, provide financial support, or give many other benefits. Your partner cares about you largely for what you bring to the relationship, not who you are as an individual or your needs as a separate human being.

- Your partner might resent your attempts at trying to fulfill your human potential or balance in life. Your partner might be critical or even punitive of the time and effort you spend trying to meet your personal needs if they are not the same as his or hers. Your partner might be an impediment or detriment to fulfilling your needs, goals, or potential.

- If your partner is proud of you, it might be largely as a possession. What you bring to the relationship makes your partner look good. You make your partner look smart, rich, successful, like a good parent, like a socialite, or whatever image your partner wants you to enhance. If this is the case, your partner isn't proud of you for your personal successes; in fact, your partner might even resent them or be jealous of them. Your partner is proud only of what they mean to him or her.

- If communication has become so difficult that you cannot see a possible solution on your own, you and your partner might want to see a relationship counselor.

Do you want your relationship to improve? Discuss this with your partner and determine whether your partner is willing to work with you to improve the relationship. If your partner is willing to change and improve his or her behavior, focus on the Relationship Rights that have the most negative scores and how you and your partner can improve the scores. You might want to seek counseling or professional help to assist you as you work through each of these areas. You might need to go back to the Partners' Starting Agreement. Make sure you and your partner both accept the agreement that you are each individual human beings with rights that must be respected.

If your partner is unwilling to discuss or acknowledge the real problems in your relationship, as shown in your Relationship Reality Check, you might want to seek individual help to look at your options. If your score was strongly negative in the Red Rights areas of Hurtful Physical or Sexual Behaviors or Threats, you might want to enlist outside help rather than confronting your partner by yourself. Your safety, and the safety of your children, is the most important thing. Pay special attention to Chapter Twelve, "How Far Is Too Far?"

Chapter Eleven

REMEMBER, RELATIONSHIPS WORK TWO WAYS!

Asking Questions of Ourselves

Now that you have finished your scoring, try to get a picture of the whole relationship. Remember, you need to support your partner's rights while having your rights supported by your partner. Neither partner in a mutual relationship can expect to have all their rights supported at the expense of the other. Be honest with yourself as to how much you give to the relationship and how you support your partner. Then look at the relationship from your partner's perspective.

Being honest with yourself means looking at how much of yourself you actively give to support your partner and the relationship.

It's often easy to criticize our partners without realistically looking at ourselves. Sometimes we keep giving and giving into what turns out to be a black hole, where the more we do for our partner, the more our partner wants. There is no end to what is expected of us, and even then, our partner is never satisfied. Our partners say, "If you just do this one thing, then everything will be good." So we do that "one thing" and then everything still isn't good; our partner wants "another thing" and "another thing" and "another thing." Nothing seems to make our partners happy.

[153]

On the other hand, there may be things we do, that may be hurtful and unsupportive. These may be things we do either consciously or unconsciously that we don't realize are so hurtful. Now is the time to take a look at our own actions.

What actions do you take to show support for your partner's Green Rights?
- How do you show your partner that you support his or her interests, opinions, time, space, development, and other personal rights?
- Can you list the ways you support your partner?
- Does your partner recognize or appreciate what you do?
- Does your partner take your efforts and actions for granted?
- Are there things you do to deny or control your partner's Green Rights either consciously or unconsciously?
- Do you sometimes resent your partner's Green Rights? Do you show it or let your partner know in other ways?

Does your partner benefit from being in the relationship with you or could your partner just as well be living with a roommate or a family member?
- What benefits do you give to your partner for being in the relationship?
- Do you go out of your way to make your partner feel good about being with you? How?
- Do you treat your partner like a friend or special person? How do you make your partner feel special?
- Do you take your relationship for granted? If so, why? What can you do differently?

Based on your actions, should your partner feel safe with you?
- Why should your partner feel safe both physically and emotionally around you? Or why not?
- Do you feel you have a right to control your partner and/or that your partner should be obedient and submissive to you?
- Do you do things that may hurt your partner? What are they?
- Before you act, do you think about how your actions will make your partner feel?
- Do you really care about how your partner feels or are you more concerned about doing whatever you want?

- Are you more concerned about getting your partner to do what you want than how you treat your partner?
- Do you always have to be right at the expense of your partner?
- Do you accept your partner's differences or do you think you have a right to make your partner change?
- Do you feel you have a right to criticize or punish your partner when your partner makes a mistake or doesn't do what you expect?
- Are you conscious of the tone of voice or gestures you use with your partner? How do you think they make your partner feel?
- Do you feel you have the right to constantly complain regardless of how it makes others feel?
- When you are upset, are you able to control your actions toward your partner? Do you take responsibility for what you do to your partner?

Looking at your relationship from your partner's perspective means stepping out of your shoes and into your partner's head.

That does not mean necessarily thinking as your partner would think, since we are all different. But instead, knowing your partner as you do, what do you think your partner is really feeling? Why do you think your partner acts as he or she does? As we said at the beginning, people often have different definitions for relationships or different ideas for being a successful partner. Based on your partner's actions, do you think your partner has a different definition or expectation of your relationship than you? As you answer the following questions, look at your partner's actions and think about your partner's expectations for the relationship.

How do you think your partner would say that you support his or her rights?
- If your partner marked his or her Relationship Scale, how do you think you would be scored in supporting each of your partner's rights?
- Is your partner correct?
- Does your partner expect too much? Is your partner one-sided? Or is your partner realistic?

How do you think your partner would say he or she supports each of your rights?

- If your partner marked your Relationship Scale for you, how do you think your partner would mark each of your rights (in terms of how he or she supports them)?
- Why do you think your partner would say this?
- Is your partner right? Why or why not?
- Do you think your partner is aware of your rights?
- Do you think your partner cares about your rights?
- Do you think your partner is aware of how he or she makes you feel about each of your rights?
- Does your partner think he or she is a good partner? Why?

After answering the above questions do you feel you have a mutually supportive relationship? Why or why not?

In a healthy, mutually supportive relationship, both partners' Relationship Rights scores are on the positive side. For one partner to have a "plus" ten score doesn't mean the other partner has to have a "minus" ten. Both partners can enhance and support each other.

If you look at or imagine both your partner's and your Relationship Scale scores, would they both be on the positive side? Or would one be on the positive side at the expense of the other? Or would they both be on the negative side, because one partner is upset that the other partner isn't subservient, under control, or doing enough? How do you support each other as partners?

SLOW DOWN FOR THIS EXTRA THOUGHT

For one partner to be positive, the other doesn't have to be negative.

For one partner to be supported, the other doesn't have to be denied or controlled.

For one partner to grow, the other doesn't have to be held back or regress.

For one partner to be a +10, the other doesn't have to be –10.

A great relationship can be a 10/10 for both partners—or at least a goal.

Chapter Twelve

HOW FAR IS TOO FAR?

Where Do Behaviors Cross the Line?

Have your partner's behaviors crossed the line? Knowing when your partner's behaviors have gone too far is, unfortunately, not simple—it's often confusing. The situation gets complicated because you love your partner and are trying to please him or her (and your family) at the same time you are trying to fulfill yourself as an individual. You continually try to satisfy conflicting priorities. It's confusing. Which priority takes precedence? At what point does pleasing your partner diminish you too much as an individual?

Also, sometimes a partner changes during the relationship. Perhaps your partner treated you one way at the beginning of your relationship but now is treating you differently. You still see your partner as the original person you fell in love with, but he or she has turned into another person. Sometimes people change when they say "I do," or sometimes they change at a major life passage such as childbirth, midlife, a medical crisis, or a job loss. A partner who changes color toward you without warning is a relationship chameleon.

RELATIONSHIP CHAMELEON

A relationship chameleon is a partner whose color changes at some point in the relationship, never to return to the original state. A chameleon changes behavior toward you but makes you believe the change is supposed to happen or that it is your fault. You may feel that if you just acted differently, the original color you knew will return. But the truth is that the chameleon's new color is permanent, and no matter how much more you give or tolerate, you can do nothing to change it back. Your partner has to want to change. You can't do it.

Because recognizing abusive behaviors when you are so close to the other person is difficult, you need to know when your rights should take priority. You need a simple guideline to recognize when your partner's behaviors or demands have gone too far and your rights are being violated.

People toss around the term "abuse." Most of us certainly don't want to think that we allow ourselves to be abused, but if you've lost the qualities that make you a human being and you're not being treated as one, what can be worse?

Unfortunately, "abuse" has become a nebulous term that covers a wide range of behaviors. Abuse can be anything from stepping on someone's toes to beating a person into submission. We need to know when a behavior crosses the line and becomes abuse. Culturally, we call it abuse only when the behavior becomes severe and physical, but by then it might be too late.

We all might have hurt someone's feelings at one time or another. We all make mistakes. We're not perfect. Doing something hurtful and later feeling remorse and asking for forgiveness is not abuse.

However, someone who believes these hurtful behaviors are justified or someone who has a repeated pattern of hurtful behaviors has crossed the line into abuse. That person has no remorse or empathy for the partner. Even after apologies, the behaviors continue. When there is a continuation of small but regular hurtful behaviors or an attitude that you're in some way a lesser human being, your partner has crossed the line into abuse. Your partner is not attempting to control his or her hurtful behaviors. At that point, your partner is violating your rights as a human being. When human rights are routinely denied through your partner's behavior, that behavior is abusive. Routine violation of Green or Red Rights is abuse.

OUR DEFINITION OF ABUSE

***Abuse is any regular pattern of behaviors that denies a
person's Personal Rights (Green) or Safety Rights (Red).***

Abuse usually occurs in an escalating cycle. The more rights you allow your partner to deny or control, the more you are telling your partner the behavior is okay. As long as you don't yell or say "Stop," your partner will likely continue the behavior because you allow it and he or she can get away with it. At this point, you need to go back to the Partners' Starting Agreement and say, "I am an individual human being, and I deserve to be treated that way!" This should help you realize that you are no longer obligated to please your partner because he or she demands too much.

The first step in stopping abuse is recognizing it. If your partner does not respect your rights as an individual human being, you can now name and claim your Relationship Rights for yourself. When your rights are denied in your relationship, state loudly, **"STOP! That's abuse, and I'm not going to take it anymore."**

WHY DOES YOUR PARTNER HURT YOU? AND WHY DOESN'T YOUR PARTNER SEEM TO UNDERSTAND?

Unfortunately, your partner might not be able to stop the abuse, even when he or she professes to love you. Often your partner might not know that his or her behaviors are abusive or might believe that the behaviors toward you are justified and acceptable. Despite continual attempts at trying to make your partner understand your hurt, something seems to be wrong in the communications process.

- Instead of being understanding when you tell your partner to stop, he or she might become defensive about the behaviors, try to justify them, or blame you for causing them.
- You might repeatedly try to communicate your feelings to your partner, but he or she just doesn't seem to understand.
- At the beginning of the relationship everything was great; now your partner doesn't seem to understand or care about how you feel.
- You might become frustrated at being made to feel that you are a bad communicator or that you are crazy.
- Sometimes, your partner might seem to understand and apologize for hurtful behaviors, but the behaviors still continue. Your partner does nothing to change.

- You might feel like you and your partner are speaking different languages.

In truth, that might be exactly the case—you and your partner aren't speaking the same relationship language. Or, if your partner changes colors like a relationship chameleon, your partner's relationship language might have changed as well.

Take this first-hand example from Beth.

ARE YOU AND YOUR PARTNER SPEAKING DIFFERENT LANGUAGES?

When I was a young graduate student in business administration, I went on an exchange program to one of the large car manufacturers in Japan. My job was to help analyze the company's marketing programs and periodically check out those of its competitors. Although the job didn't appear that unusual on the outside, it brought me many cultural challenges as a young woman in the conservative, male business world of 1970's Japan.

One day my bosses sent me to Tokyo to review the grand unveiling of their major competitor's new car model. The competitor's claim was that this new car would make you feel happy and "up." Their multimillion-yen advertising and marketing campaign focused on this claim. On the surface the idea sounded wonderful.

As I walked into their largest dealership in Japan, I was prepared to see pictures of smiles and faces of happy people. Instead, everywhere I looked I saw signs, banners, balloons, and sales brochures saying "Up You." And each salesperson wore a lapel button proudly proclaiming, "Up You." All around the dealership, everywhere I looked, were the words "Up You," "Up You," and more "Up You." I then went to the Ginza, the busiest street corner in the world, the Times Square of Japan, and it was flashing on and off in bright lights, in the biggest letters imaginable, "Up You," "Up You," "Up You," again and again and again. Needless to say, I was horrified.

I went back to my office the next day to report my official findings to my bosses. How does a twenty-three-year-old American woman diplomatically describe the meaning of "up you" to her conservative, proper, older Japanese male bosses? Well, I did it with great care, and they still gasped. These proper men could hardly believe their ears. Then they huddled for a while and decided they should call their competitors and tell them the real meaning of their new advertising campaign.

They didn't hear from the competitors for several days. Finally, one afternoon they got a call from the competitor's president. He politely thanked them for their call and concern. He then carefully explained that his company would do nothing to change its slogan because the slogan wasn't in "English" but in "Japanese English" and "Up You" has a different meaning in "Japanese English."

Now ask yourself whether you and your partner are speaking the same language. If your partner tells you "Up you!" will you feel up and happy or hurt and insulted? Do you and your partner articulate the same meanings when you communicate? Do you and your partner have the same relationship expectations? If you aren't understanding each other when you try to communicate, you might not realize that you are speaking different relationship languages. This is similar to the different definitions of "love" and "relationship" we gave you at the beginning of the book—same words, different meanings.

Does your partner say one thing but then treat you differently? For example, does your partner tell you how wonderful you are and then treat you like a servant or slave? Does your partner profess to love you but make you feel like an old rag picked up and used whenever it's wanted and then tossed back in a corner and forgotten? Or does your partner tell you that you are the most special person on earth and then treat you as though you are the most special person on earth?

The relationship language you and your partner speak depends on what you and your partner were taught in childhood or your prior relationship expectations. Your partner might not comprehend or believe his or her behaviors are hurtful or abusive, even when you say so. You hear your partner say, "I love you" and can't understand why your partner hurts you and what's wrong. Then when you try to communicate, nothing seems to work. It sounds as though you're speaking the same language, but you're not. Something doesn't feel right, but you can't explain it. You need to recognize that you're not speaking the same relationship language, even though you might be saying the same words.

Once partners realize there are different languages and other alternatives to their definition of a "successful partner," they can look at relationship expectations and behaviors with other options for success. Then, partners can realize they may live the relationship language they choose. A partner can decide to learn a different language and move beyond family teachings, other past experiences, or prior expectations.

Partners can learn a new relationship language with a new starting agreement rather than the one they learned from their past. The relationship language your partner's parents used was fine for them, but it doesn't have to be the same for you. You and your partner can choose a relationship language that is right for you—one that is based on honoring and respecting each other as separate individuals, yet coming together and sharing as intimate partners. We have a choice. We can become multilingual to understand each other better.

Patricia Evans describes the mutual understanding required for relationships in her book *The Verbally Abusive Relationship* (Adams Media Corporation, 1996). We have recommended it to others who, like us, have needed to understand the differences between themselves and their partners. The book emphasizes the importance of both partners coming to the relationship as separate people who respect each other as individuals.

SLOW DOWN FOR THIS EXTRA THOUGHT

To bring one's thoughts and to hear the other's,
To express one's enthusiasm and to delight in the other's,
To reveal one's self and to reflect the other,
To value one's self and to esteem the other,
To enjoy one's creations and to treasure the other's,
To pursue one's growth and to nurture the other's,
To cherish one's solitude and to honor the other's,
To follow one's interests and to encourage the other,
To act at one's pace and to accept the other's,
To indulge one's self and to assist the other,
To protect one's self and to comfort the other,
To see one's self and to behold the other,
To be one's self and to let the other be,
Is to love one's self and to love the other.

PART THREE

ADDITIONAL HELP—

HELP YOURSELF, WORK WITH YOUR PARTNER, OR ASK A COUNSELOR

Chapter Thirteen

THE WRITE THING

JOURNALING IDEAS

Writing in a journal can be an excellent tool for further exploring the results of your Relationship Reality Check. It can validate each of your scores by providing more clarity about the reasons behind your thoughts and feelings. This organization of your thoughts can also pave the way for you to share the insights of your Relationship Reality Check with your partner.

If you would like to consider writing in a journal, this section will give you ideas. However, writing is only an aid—it is not necessary to complete your Relationship Reality Check. If you would like to consider journaling read this chapter.

WHY SHOULD I WRITE IN A JOURNAL? IT SOUNDS LIKE A LOT OF WORK!

Yes, we will admit it right up front—writing is work. But we all know deep inside that anything worthwhile is work. Take a look at this old saying: "There are always two choices, two paths to take. One is easy, and its only reward is that it's easy." If you didn't care about your relationship and weren't willing to put in some work, you probably wouldn't have bought this book. So what are the benefits of writing about your relationship as you travel down your Relationship Road?

Writing in a journal can give you the opportunity for personal growth. Writing requires that you take time alone to think about things. It presents you with a wonderful opportunity to sort things out in your head and to understand them. At times it requires that you think about things objectively; at other times, the only thing that's important is how you feel. Writing can help you find clarity in your private thoughts and feelings and can help you decide what things are important and what things are not.

Writing in a journal can give you the opportunity to communicate with your partner. Writing doesn't just give you the opportunity for introspection; it also presents an opportunity to act on the insights and knowledge you have gained. You might gain a new perspective from your writing that is so enlightening you might decide to share it with your partner. If you do, the thoughts and feelings you have organized on paper will be easier to verbalize and communicate in a nonthreatening and positive way. If you decide to use your writing to communicate with your partner, you can find help later in this chapter under the heading "Suggestions for Sharing Your Relationship Reality Check with Your Partner." Even if you don't decide to share your writing with your partner, you will know what you would say if you were given the opportunity.

Writing in a journal can help you decide what you want to do about your relationship. You really have only three choices when dealing with a relationship: keep it the way it is, try to fix it, or end it. And yet, in the midst of the feelings that go along with relationships, you might not be able to see this clearly. You might feel that you have many choices and things to consider, and you just can't decide which is best. You might feel that you have no choices and could then become paralyzed by this thought. Either scenario leads to frustration and a sense of being overwhelmed with too few or too many choices. Writing in a journal can help clear your mind, help you identify the real feelings and problems, and help you set and prioritize relationship goals. "Clearing the fog" can help you see your relationship choices and enable you to think creatively so that you can move forward.

BEFORE YOU START TO JOURNAL

Before you begin writing, reflect on your and your partner's expectations for a relationship:

- What did you believe your role was to be in your relationship? How did you expect to be treated?
- Based on what you have seen, what role do you think your partner expected to have in the relationship? How do you think your partner expects to treat you?
- Do your expectations match? Why or why not?

HOW TO WRITE IN A JOURNAL

Now that you have learned about your Green, Yellow, and Red Rights and evaluated them with your Relationship Reality Check, you have the opportunity to think about the reasons behind your scores with the writing activities that follow. We encourage you to buy a notebook or even a nice blank book in which to do your writing.

The writing activities are designed to give you the opportunity to understand your feelings on a deeper level. But the activities will also present an opportunity to problem-solve and think creatively about how you could improve a particular area in your relationship. The activities are written in general language, but you can adapt the activities by inserting the name of specific rights.

You don't have to do all the activities. You don't have to write about all your rights. You can pick and choose. Take your time with each activity you decide to do, and work at your own speed. Writing helps some people clear confusion, but don't be afraid to walk away from the activities if you are feeling stumped or frustrated. Come back when you feel less confused. Be honest. Write everything down that comes to mind—good, bad, or ugly. Don't worry about grammar, spelling, or anything else that might keep you from pouring your thoughts onto a piece of paper. If you are worried about privacy, take whatever steps are necessary to ensure that your journal remains private.

Keep at it. Writing, and the self-discovery that comes with it, is like a spiral staircase that continues upward until you get to your destination. The rewards come with time and each step you take.

EXAMPLES OF JOURNALING ACTIVITIES

General:
1. List at least two examples to support your scoring of each right.
2. How did each of these examples make you feel?

Green Rights:
1. Give two examples of things you do to support your partner's expression or development of each Green Right.
2. Do you think your partner is aware of your efforts? Why or why not?
3. Now list two examples of things your partner could do differently to support each of your Green Rights, where applicable.

Yellow Rights:
1. Do you and your partner support this Yellow Right for each other?
2. How do you support it?
3. How does your partner support it?
4. Would you like your partner to do something differently? If so, what?

Red Rights:
1. Does it appear that your partner tries to manage or take responsibility for his or her behaviors in support of this Red Right? Why or why not? (Give specific examples when possible.)
2. If applicable, list ways your partner could have acted differently to make you feel better.

Communications:
1. How does your partner's support or denial of each right affect your communication and your relationship?
2. Is there something your partner could do differently that could improve communications?

SUGGESTIONS FOR SHARING YOUR RELATIONSHIP REALITY CHECK WITH YOUR PARTNER (IF YOU DECIDE TO DO SO)

The goal of any assessment is to obtain information and then to do something with it. By doing a Relationship Reality Check, you have done a lot of introspective work, and hopefully you now have new information and insights into yourself and your relationship. What you do with this information is up to you. If you decide you want to keep this to yourself for your own understanding, that's okay. If you would like to share it with your partner, you may use some of the following suggestions to open communication and begin your discussions.

- Don't feel obligated to show your partner your Relationship Reality Check. This is your reality check based on *your* feelings. It belongs to you. Only share this if you feel safe, if you will not be criticized or ridiculed, and if your partner wants to work on improving the whole relationship. Or show it to your partner if you have both done Relationship Reality Checks and want to share them to work together on improving your relationship.

- If you choose to share your Relationship Reality Check with your partner, you should do it in an open and communicative way that is motivated by a desire to improve and grow, not attack, belittle, criticize, or berate.

- Don't just share the problems; share the good feelings, too. Try to encourage more of this happiness by telling your partner how good he or she makes you feel.

- Have your discussion in a quiet environment without the interruption of phone calls, friends, or children.

- Prioritize! Don't try to solve all your problems at once. Discuss your greatest concerns. You might not have time for everything in one session, and/or your whole list might seem overwhelming and could put your partner on the defensive. Solving a few problems at a time is much easier than risking feeling overwhelmed by all of them at once.

- Use your Reality Check journaling as an outline for your discussions. Your writing should highlight your feelings: why you feel as you do, how you try to treat your partner, how you feel your partner treats you, and how you would like your partner to treat you. Share with your partner any specific suggestions regarding what you would like him or her to do and how that behavior will make you feel as a person.

- When you tell your partner that you have concerns about your relationship, make sure that you are safe, both emotionally and physically. Make sure that your partner will not hurt you for expressing your concerns.

- You might want to start by showing your partner the Partners' Starting Agreement and seeing if he or she agrees: "Both partners in a relationship are individual human beings and deserve to be treated that way." If you and your partner don't share this agreement, your partner might not understand why you feel as you do. Remember that the Starting Agreement is the foundation for all the Green, Yellow, and Red Rights.

- If your partner is receptive, you might want to share the Partners' Starting Agreement and the Relationship Guide. They highlight both partners' rights in the relationship. They may also be used if you choose to go into counseling together.

SLOW DOWN FOR THIS EXTRA THOUGHT

GUIDELINES FOR COMMUNICATION:

1. *Make "I" statements ("I feel..."). "You" statements are often blaming and get nowhere.*

2. *Listen to your partner; don't be thinking of what you're going to say next. Repeat what you heard so that your partner knows you were listening.*

3. *Don't give double messages; don't say one thing with your words and express something totally different with your tone of voice. Said sarcastically, "Sure you can go" has the opposite meaning of the words alone.*

4. *How a person feels about something can't be argued about.*

5. *Don't use generalizations such as "always" or "never."*

6. *Try to put yourself in your partner's shoes when he or she talks about feelings.*

7. *Watch out for guilt trips.*

Chapter Fourteen

IF YOU WANT TO WORK WITH A COUNSELOR OR THERAPIST

Not All Therapists Are Alike

Therapists can be helpful to couples when working through relationship problems. They can act as professionals and unbiased third parties to help solve conflicts and improve relationships. They can also help you make decisions about your relationship: whether you want your relationship to improve, stay the same, or end. Even if your relationship is to end, you still might need a good therapist to help you and your partner dissolve your relationship as smoothly as possible. This approach is especially important if you have children.

However, as helpful as therapists can be in a relationship, beware—not all therapists are equally helpful. We, as well as many others, have found that some therapists, and the treatment they provide, can even be hurtful. There are different kinds of therapists coming from various backgrounds with many kinds of credentials and a wide range of experience. A degree behind a name or a shingle on the door stating "Marriage Therapist" does not necessarily qualify a therapist to give you the type or quality of help you are looking for.

Not all therapists look at both partners in a relationship as individual human beings deserving of the same rights. Unfortunately, therapists are human, too, and so might be biased. Roadblocks might be hidden inside a therapist's office that could keep you from getting the specific help your relationship needs. As people who have been to many different types of relationship therapists and have friends who have had similar experiences, we can tell you that you should select your therapist carefully. The wrong selection could actually prolong a bad situation or make you believe hurtful behaviors are acceptable. If your gut feeling is that your partner's behaviors are hurting you as an individual and you leave your therapist's office feeling "crazy" or even more confused than when you walked in, your therapist might not be tackling the problems with an unbiased approach.

We don't pretend to be therapists, but we sure do have experience as "therapeutees," and we can tell you what has worked and what hasn't worked—for us. Here is a list of warning signs that might help you and your relationship get the kind of unbiased help that you need:

Be wary of a family therapist or marriage counselor who . . .

- has preset, stereotyped role models for men and women (this person lacks the ability to see you as a unique individual)
- does not agree that both partners are equal human beings in the relationship and share the same Relationship Rights (this person may show bias from the beginning)
- insists on therapy sessions only with both partners meeting together, rather than some individual sessions and some together as a couple—especially necessary when either of the partners requests a meeting alone or feels unsafe (this may expose you to unnecessary retaliation or withholding)
- minimizes your feelings (this lacks sensitivity to your position and acceptance of your feelings)
- doesn't acknowledge anything you say as relevant to the problems or issues (this lacks openness to both sides)
- doesn't ask questions of *both* partners or encourage both partners to talk, share, and be open and honest (this looks at the relationship with unbalanced input)
- states that partners should be accepted as they are, even if their behaviors are hurtful, and then tells you that your choice is to accept your partner's hurtful behaviors or leave the relationship rather than speak out and state that the behaviors are hurtful, disrespectful and unacceptable in a mutually supportive relationship (this person is unwilling to speak out against abusive behaviors, telling you that it is your choice to leave, but that your partner's behaviors are okay as long as you are not physically hurt)

- does most of the talking (this makes you wonder whether you were really heard or will be able to express yourself)
- insists on evaluating a partner's "at home" behavior based on the partner's behavior in the therapist's office (this person appears ignorant to the fact that your partner is on "best behavior")
- insists that all relationship problems are two-sided and suggests that you did something to create your partner's behavior (while there may be reasons you tolerated your partner's behavior, it doesn't mean you created or deserved it)
- does not end each session with a respectful resolution for both partners (if partners leave with open issues discussed in session, they are often in a more difficult or dangerous position than before they came in)
- claims confidentiality conflicts and will only take on one of the partners as a client, so the therapist hears about the relationship from only one side (that's like a judge hearing from only the prosecution and not the defense who still renders a verdict claiming, "It's fair")

    If a partner is in individual therapy and also needs marriage counseling, he or she should be told to go to a separate marriage counselor if confidentiality is required. At the same time, the therapist should refrain from making judgments about the partner or giving advice about the relationship unless the counselor also meets separately with the other partner to hear the other side.

Here are some of our recommendations for selecting a therapist and integrating your Relationship Reality Check with therapy:

- Begin your search for a therapist much like you would for a doctor, dentist, or attorney. Call a local referral agency or professional organization or seek out friends who might have names of therapists they have used. If the name is a referral from friends, be sure to ask whether they were comfortable with the therapist's personality or style and whether they were happy or unhappy with the results of the therapy. If they were unhappy, ask why.
- Once you have several names, interview the therapists, preferably in person or at least over the phone. Make sure that you feel comfortable with this person and the way he/she listens, the way he/she responds, and his/her recommended approach to your relationship situation before you commit to working with him or her. Make a list of questions ahead of time. Ask for references. Ask about educational background, years of experience, and any professional organizations the therapist belongs to. It's your life, it's your experience, it's your choice. Take your time and choose carefully.

- Don't forget to ask general questions about price, billing and payment procedures, cancellation policies, and whether your insurance benefits will cover your sessions. You might also want to ask about the therapist's availability in the event of a crisis situation or emergency.
- If you are a victim of verbal, emotional, physical, or sexual abuse, be open and honest about it with the therapist. It is important that the therapist understands that safety is an issue and that it could become an even bigger issue at home after a session in which you have expressed your feelings. Ask your therapist for some suggestions for staying safe at home, and implement them.
- If you want the therapist to use *Relationship Rights (and wrongs)* in your therapy sessions as a reference resource, introduce it early.
- Ask the therapist to read the Partners' Starting Agreement and the Relationship Guide and ask whether he or she will support them in your therapy.
- Ask the therapist whether he or she is willing to ask for an agreement between you and your partner as the basis for your therapy at your first session. This agreement is the Partners' Starting Agreement: "Both partners in a relationship are individual human beings who have the same human rights. Both partners deserve to be treated like individuals even though they are in a relationship." Will the therapist have everyone sign the Bill of Relationship Rights at this session?
- Emphasize that after any disagreement or discussion of Relationship Rights, the Partners' Starting Agreement should always be revisited. How does a behavior make the other partner feel as an individual? Have both partners measure their behaviors on the Relationship Scale so they can discuss and understand what they are doing to each other (remembering that violation of Red Rights is heavier than Green or Yellow Rights).
- Ask the therapist whether you can discuss the Relationship Guide and your Relationship Rights in therapy sessions. Explain that you need a safe environment in which to express your feelings to your partner.
- Ask whether the therapist will help your partner understand these Relationship Rights and help you express your feelings regarding them.
- Explain to the therapist that one of the reasons you want to use the Partners' Starting Agreement and the Relationship Guide is because it's helpful to have benchmarks and language to help express yourself. Feel free to tell the therapist that you need encouragement, support, and a positive environment in order to be able to express yourself openly and accurately.

- Ask the therapist some of the questions above, such as how he or she holds the sessions. Will you be able to meet alone as well as together? Does the therapist have group support sessions available? Will the therapist be willing to speak out or does the therapist believe that you just need to accept a partner's hurtful behaviors or leave? Does the therapist advocate mutually supportive, negotiated relationships? Do you feel a comfort level with this therapist?

Above all, if you have decided to bring a therapist into your relationship, please try to make the following commitments and ask your partner to make them as well:

- Make the commitment of TIME. Regardless of the condition of your relationship, it took time to get where you are, and it will take time to get where you want to be.
- Make the commitment of EFFORT. Working with a relationship therapist takes the effort and dedication of both partners. If only one partner is committed to the relationship and the work of the relationship, you might be spinning your wheels in endless frustration and you might need to talk to your therapist about more realistic expectations and outcomes.
- Make a commitment to REALISM. Be realistic about the help your relationship might or might not be getting from the therapy. A therapist is not a miracle worker, and therapy is not a cure-all. You can set and reset expectations and goals several times during the course of therapy, but someone might have to say at some point, "Enough is enough." Don't be afraid to say "This isn't working" and make a different plan.

APPENDIX A

Resources and Referrals

The first step to solving any problem or improving any situation is to have information. After working through your Relationship Reality Check, you probably have information about the health and condition of your personal life and relationship that you didn't have before. Quite possibly you had a sense or a gut feeling about your relationship, but now that you have calculated your score and evaluated it, you have new information that you'll want to put to use.

Depending upon the result of your Relationship Reality Check, you might feel that you need to contact outside or professional help for your relationship, yourself, your partner, or your children. This section is designed to try to help you with those efforts. As you use this section, please remember:

- **This is just a starting point.** This resource and referral section is full of addresses and phone numbers for national self-help organizations, support groups, hotlines, statistics, and checklists that might provide additional help to you. It is meant to be a resource that can aid you in finding the help you and your family might need.

- **Be your own detective.** Programs and organizations are constantly changing and growing, so we encourage you to be aggressive and resourceful when using the information in these pages. The information was self-reported by individuals and from a variety of sources. If you have comments or discover additional resources that you feel would be beneficial to others in your situation, please let us know (see the back of this book on how to contact us).

- **These are not endorsements or recommendations.** *Relationship Rights (and wrongs)* and its authors do not recommend or endorse specific organizations or services found in this resource section.

NATIONAL RESOURCES AND HELP HOTLINES

The following are a suggested list of resources to contact for specific problem areas. Please note that phones numbers, addresses, and email addresses change. These are the contacts listed at the time of writing. You may want to double-check the contact numbers or e-mail addresses at the time of your reading the book.

DOMESTIC AND CHILD ABUSE

CHILD ABUSE HOTLINE (twenty four-hours)
(800) 792-5200
Support and information.

NATIONAL CHILD ABUSE HOTLINE
(800) 422-4453
http://nccanch.acf.hhs.gov
Help and information.

YOUTH CRISIS HOTLINE
(800) HIT-HOME
(800) 448-4663
(800) 621-4000 (for runaways)
www.1800hithome.com
Hotline for reporting child abuse and help for runaways.

NATIONAL DOMESTIC VIOLENCE HOTLINE
(800) 799-SAFE
(800) 799-7233
www.ncadv.org
Twenty-four-hour hotline that offers crisis intervention, problem-solving skills, support, and referrals to victims of domestic violence, their families, friends, and perpetrators. Provides bilingual (English and Spanish) advocates and translation services at all times. Serves all fifty states, the Commonwealth of Puerto Rico, and the Virgin Islands. Callers also can get information and referrals for local shelters, support groups, and crisis intervention help.

MEN'S/FATHER'S HOTLINE
(512) 472-DADS/(512) 472-3237
807 Brazos, Suite 315
Austin, Texas 78701
www.menweb.org
National hotline and crisis line for men and fathers. Callers are referred to local, state, or national assistance programs that can help them solve their problems.

NATIONAL CLEARINGHOUSE ON CHILD ABUSE AND NEGLECT INFORMATION
(800) FYI-3366; 703-385-7565
P.O. Box 1182
Washington, DC 20013-1182

NATIONAL COUNCIL ON CHILD ABUSE AND FAMILY VIOLENCE
(800) 222-2000; (202) 429-6695
1155 Connecticut Avenue, NW, Suite 400
Washington, DC 20036

PARENTS STRESS HOTLINE
(800) 632-8188
Help for parents.

SEXUAL ASSAULT CRISIS LINE
(800) 643-6250
(800) 656-HOPE

NATIONAL ORGANIZATION AGAINST MALE SEXUAL VICTIMIZATION
(800) 738-4181; (614) 445-8283
P.O. Box 40055
St. Paul, MN 55104
Founded in 1985. Information and referrals to local resources for male survivors of sexual assault. Newsletter.

PARENTS ANONYMOUS
(909) 621-6184; (909) 625-6304 fax
www.parentsanonymous.org
675 W. Foothill Blvd., #220
Claremont, CA 91711-3475
Nationally 2,300 groups. Founded in 1970. Professionally facilitated peer-led group for parents who are having difficulty and would like to learn more effective ways of raising their children.

BATTERED WOMEN'S JUSTICE PROJECT
(800) 903-0111; (218) 722-1545 fax
Minnesota Program Development, Inc.
2206 West 4th Street
Duluth, MN 55806
www.bwjp.org

CENTER FOR THE PREVENTION OF SEXUAL AND DOMESTIC VIOLENCE
(206) 634-1903; (206) 634-0115
1914 North 34th Street, Suite 105
Seattle, WA 98103
www.cpsdr.org
Excellent links to other violence prevention organizations.

NATIONAL RESOURCE CENTER ON DOMESTIC VIOLENCE
(800) 537-2238; (717) 545-9456 fax
6400 Flank Drive, Suite 1300
Harrisburg, PA 17112
www.nrcdv.org

INCEST RESOURCES, INC.
46 Pleasant St.
Cambridge, MA 02139
Founded in 1980. Provides educational and resource materials for female and male survivors and for professionals working with survivors. For complete information send S.A.S.E. with two first class stamps.

PARENTS UNITED INTERNATIONAL, INC.
(209) 572-3446; (209) 524-7780 fax
615 15th Street
Modesto, CA 95354-2510
Nationally fifty-five chapters. Founded in 1972. Provides treatment for child sexual abuse. Includes individual therapy, group therapy, and guided self-help. Also for adults molested as children.

SURVIVORS OF INCEST ANONYMOUS
(410) 282-3400, (410) 893-3322
(410) 282-3400 fax
P.O. Box 21817
Baltimore, MD 21222
www.siawso.org
Internationally five hundred groups. Founded in 1982. Self-help twelve-step program for men and women eighteen years or older who have been victims of child sexual abuse and want to be survivors. Newsletter and literature. Send self-addressed envelope when writing.

DRUG AND ALCOHOL ABUSE

NATIONAL DRUG AND ALCOHOL TREATMENT REFERRAL
National Treatment Hotline
(800) 662-HELP (English)
(800) 66-AYUDA (Spanish)
(800) 228-0427 (TDD)
www.niaaa.nih.gov
Help in finding treatment options in your state; support and information regarding drug treatment referrals, alcohol problems, or adolescent or family problems within local communities.

NATIONAL COUNCIL ON ALCOHOLISM HELP LINE
1-(800)-NCA-CALL
AL-ANON and Alateen
(888) 425-2666
http://www.al-anon-alateen.org
Worldwide organization that offers a self-help recovery program for families and friends.

ALCOHOLICS ANONYMOUS (AA) WORLD SERVICES
(212) 870-3400
475 Riverside Drive
New York, NY 10015
www.alcoholics-anonymous.org

COCAINE ANONYMOUS (NATIONAL REFERRAL LINE)
(800) 347-8998
3740 Overland Avenue, Suite G
Los Angeles, CA 90034
www.ca.org

MARIJUANNA ANONYMOUS
(800) 766-6779
P.O. Box 2912
Van Nuys, CA 91404
www.marijuanna-anonymous.org

NATIONAL ASSOCIATION FOR CHILDREN OF ALCOHOLICS
(301) 468-0985
11426 Rockville Pike, Suite 100
Rockville, MD 20852
www.nacoa.org

NATIONAL CLEARINGHOUSE FOR ALCOHOL AND DRUG INFORMATION
(800) 729-6686
P.O. Box 2345
Rockville, MD 20852
www.health.org
World's largest resource for current information and materials concerning substance abuse.

NATIONAL COUNCIL ON ALCOHOL AND DRUG DEPENDENCE
(800) 622-2255; (202) 737-8122
1511 K. Street, NW
Suite 926
Washington, DC 20005
www.ncadd.org

MENTAL HEALTH

SUICIDE AND CRISIS SERVICE (NATIONAL HOPELINE)
(800) SUICIDE; (800) 784-2433
Any kind of crisis.

ANXIETY DISORDERS ASSOCIATION OF AMERICA
(301) 231-9350; (301) 231-7392 fax
www.adaa.org
National network founded in 1980. Promotes welfare of people with phobias and related anxiety disorders. Publishes a self-help group directory.

RECOVERY
(312) 337-5661; (312) 337-5756
802 N. Dearborn St.
Chicago, Il 60610
www.recovery-inc.com
International. Seven hundred groups. A community mental health organization that offers a self-help method of will training and techniques for controlling anxiety, depression, anger, and fears.

DEPRESSION & BI-POLAR SUPPORT ALLIANCE
(800) 826-3632; (312) 642-0049; (312) 642-7243
www.dbsalliance.org
National organization founded in 1986. 275 chapters. Support and information for persons with depressive and manic-depressive illnesses.

NATIONAL ASSOCIATION OF ANOREXIA NERVOSA AND ASSOCIATED DISORDERS, INC.
(847) 831-3438
FAX: (847) 433-4632
P.O. Box 7
Highland Park, IL 60035
www.anad.org
International organization founded in 1976. Three hundred+ affiliated groups. Provides referrals to professionals, self-help groups, and a newsletter.

OVEREATERS ANONYMOUS
(505) 891-2664
P.O. Box 44020
Rio Rancho, New Mexico 87174-4020
www.overeatersanonymous.org
International group founded in 1960. Nine thousand groups. A twelve-step program to help understand and overcome compulsive eating disorders. Monthly magazine and literature.

RELATIONSHIP THERAPY

AMERICAN ASSOCIATION FOR MARRIAGE AND FAMILY THERAPY(AAMFT) - (REFERRALS)
(703) 838-9808
112 S. Alfred St.
Alexandria, VA 22314

COUPLES, FAMILIES, AND CHILDREN'S SERVICES

ALLIANCE FOR CHILDEN AND FAMILIES
(800) 221-3726
11700 W. Lake Park Drive
Milwaukee, WI 53224-3099
www.alliance1.org
An international association representing more than 350 nonprofit private human service organizations. Its members serve more than six million individuals in over eight thousand communities. The Alliance for Children and Families was formed by the 1998 merger of Family Services of America and the National Association of Homes and Services for Children. It has provided ninety years of leadership for families and children.

HELP ANOTHER PERSON

Relationships impact more than just the two partners in them. The effects of a relationship carry on through the children for generations. The kind of country and civilization we become will largely depend on the values and rights we instill in our families and children. If our relationships are healthy and we instill positive self-esteem and self-worth in our children, we will build a healthy, respectful society. If we don't respect our relationships and each other, it's reflected in the world we live in. Therefore, it is incumbent on us to develop and preserve healthy relationships and make this world a better place for all of us and future generations to live in.

As we grow through our own relationships and solve our own problems, we need to remember that there are still people who need our help. Just as I wrote this book so that my personal solutions might help others or spare them the years I spent in an abusive relationship, I hope that you too will help others. You can help in many ways:

- Share this concept of *Relationship Rights (and wrongs)* with others.
- Listen to friends when they need your help or "feel crazy and confused."
- Encourage people to feel good about themselves.
- Let people know they do not have to tolerate hurt in a relationship. They have a right to feel safe at all times.
- Give a copy of this book to a friend.
- Donate to an organization that helps people in troubled relationships or one that helps build positive ones. Organizations that help others need your support to keep their programs going.

I can recommend two organizations known for their counseling and support services.

- **Alliance for Children and Families**—an association of nonprofit, private human services organizations. It strengthens the capacity of its affiliates throughout the U.S. and Canada to advocate for children, families, and communities through its internationally recognized peer network. The Alliance provides affiliates with useful, timely information; valuable tools and templates, and high quality, customized support services to aid children and families. Alliance members annually serve more than 6 million people in more than 8,000 communities.
- **Sojourner Truth House**—a domestic abuse shelter that not only takes in women and families who have been abused but also has a Batterer's Anonymous program for men and on-going prevention programs for women and children.

If you would like to support either of these organizations, you can send a tax-deductible donation to them. You can use the donation form below for your convenience. They will personally send you back a donor recognition and confirmation for your records along with their gratitude.

● ●

○ **Alliance for Children & Families**
11700 W. Lake Park Drive
Milwaukee, WI. 53224-3099
(800) 221-3726
www.alliance1.org

○ **Sojourner Truth House**
PO Box 080319
Milwaukee, WI. 53208
(414) 643-1777
www.sojournertruthhouse. org

Make out your check to the organization(s) you would like to support and send it along with this form to the corresponding address.

Your Name _____

Address _____

City, State, & Zip Code _____

Donation $_____

● ●

DO YOU NEED A SPEAKER OR
A PROGRAM FOR YOUR GROUP?

Bring Beth to your next meeting or convention and have an exciting program for building relationships and empowering each person to become the best they can be. Good for individuals, couples, teachers, professional groups, or businesses.

To request a Speaker's Kit, send or fax your request to:

Relationship Rights (and wrongs)
10936 N. Port Washington Road #269
Mequon, WI 53092
(262) 242-7639 fax
beth@relationshiprights.com

APPENDIX B

Bibliography and Suggested Reading

Ban Breathnach, Sarah. *Simple Abundance: A Daybook of Comfort and Joy.* New York: Warner Books, 1995.

Bateson, Mary Catherine. *Composing a Life.* New York: Penguin Group, 1989.

Beattie, Melody. *Beyond Codependency and Getting Better All the Time.* New York: HarperCollins Publishers, 1989.

Beattie, Melody. *Codependent No More.* Center City, MN: Hazelden, 1987.

Bradshaw, John. *Homecoming: Reclaiming and Championing Your Inner Child.* New York: Bantam Books, 1990.

Branden, Nathaniel. *How to Raise Your Self-Esteem.* New York: Bantam, 1987.

Branden, Nathaniel. *The Six Pillars of Self-Esteem.* New York: Bantam, 1994.

Buscaglia, Leo. *Loving Each Other.* New York: Holt, Rinehart and Winston, 1984.

Carter-Scott, Cherie Ph.D. *If Life Is a Game, These Are the Rules.* New York: Broadway Books, 1998.

Chopra, Deepak. *The Path to Love: Renewing the Power of Spirit in Your Life.* New York: Harmony Books, 1997.

Covey, Stephen R. *The 7 Habits of Highly Effective People.* New York: Simon & Schuster, 1989.

DeAngelis, Barbara. *Are You the One for Me?* New York: Dell Publishing, 1992.

DeAngelis, Barbara. *Secrets about Life Every Woman Should Know.* New York: Hyperion, 1999.

Evans, Patricia. *The Verbally Abusive Relationship: How to Recognize It and How to Respond.* Holbrook, MA: Bob Adams Publishers, 1992.

Evans, Patricia. *Verbal Abuse Survivors Speak Out: On Relationship and Recovery.* Holbrook, MA: Bob Adams Publishers, 1993.

Forward, Susan. *Men Who Hate Women and the Women Who Love Them.* New York: Bantam Books, 1986.

Gibran, Kahlil. *The Prophet.* New York: Alfred A. Knopf, 1923.

Hendrix, Harville. *Getting the Love You Want.* New York: Henry Holt and Company, 1988.

Hemfelt, Dr. Robert, Dr. Frank Minirth, and Dr. Paul Meier. *Love Is a Choice.* Nashville: Thomas Nelson Publishers, 1989.

Heyn, Dalma. *Marriage Shock: The Transformation of Women into Wives.* New York: Villard, 1997.

Kivel, Paul. *Men's Work.* New York: Random House, 1992.

Lerner, Harriet Goldhor, Ph.D. *The Dance of Intimacy.* New York: Harper & Row, 1989.

Lindbergh, Anne Morrow. *Gift from the Sea.* New York: Vintage Books, 1978.

Miller, Alice. *The Drama of the Gifted Child* (original title *Prisoners of Childhood*). New York: Basic Books, 1981.

Nicarthy, Jenny. *Getting Free.* Seattle: Pepper Vine, 1986.

Norwood, Robin. *Women Who Love Too Much: When You Keep Wishing and Hoping He'll Change.* New York: Simon & Schuster, 1985.

Peck, M. Scott. *The Road Less Traveled.* New York: Simon & Schuster, 1978.

Stoop, David, and Stephen Arterburn. *The Angry Man.* Dallas: Word Publishing, 1991.

Rinck, Dr. Margaret J. *Christian Men Who Hate Women.* Grand Rapids, MI: Zondervan, 1990.

Shain, Merle. *When Lovers Are Friends.* Philadelphia & New York: J.B. Lippincott, 1978.

Sher, Barbara, with Annie Gottlieb. *Wishcraft: How to Get What You Really Want.* New York: Ballantine Books, 1979.

Viorst, Judith. *Necessary Losses.* New York: Simon & Schuster, 1986.

Wallerstein, Judith, and Sandra Blakeslee. *The Good Marriage: How and Why Love Lasts.* Boston: Houghton Mifflin, 1994.

Welwood, John. *Love and Awakening.* New York: HarperCollins Publishers, 1996.

Zukav, Gary. *The Seat of the Soul.* New York: Simon & Schuster, 1989.

INDEX

Acknowledgments

In 1992, I separated from my husband and began my search for the elements of healthy and mutually supportive relationships. I needed to understand what I could have done differently to have either have saved my marriage, communicated my feelings better, or recognized the need to separate sooner. This quest took about one year and became my personal catharsis. I then shared my concept with several marriage counselors for their comments, input, and validation. They not only validated my concept, they also asked me to write it in a generic form for professionals to see from the standpoint of a "client." I didn't take their request seriously for another five years and then friends started encouraging me to write it as well. Another five years of writing and rewriting have brought this book together.

I would like to acknowledge and thank all those people who have supported me, listened to me, encouraged me, and given me input during these years.

First and foremost, I need to thank my family for giving me wonderful role models of what a mutually supportive relationship can be—including my parents, my grandparents, and my sisters. That is not to say that all relationships are perfect and without problems. But my family demonstrated that when partners support and respect each other as individuals, relationship problems can be worked out and both partners can become better human beings and stronger for being in the relationship.

Thank you to all my friends and readers who provided input so that I could write the book. Thank you to Kathie Stolpman and the people at Sojourner Truth House, where I volunteered. You have the patience, concern, and sensitivity to care for those who are in the most difficult situations.

Thank you to marriage and family counselors Helen Jurgensen, Bill Wolfe, and Lee Raffel who were not only marriage counselors for me but muses as well. You were the ones who initially encouraged me to write the book, telling me that my concept would be helpful to others besides me.

Thank you to Dr. Jane Bluestein, who helped me through the book writing process and encouraged me to publish.

Thank you to school counselors Agie Laev and Rachel O'Neal and school principal Mike Dietz who helped my family through our difficult times. An extra word of praise goes to Agie who was the only person alive to make it through the whole long first version of the book—and she did this while she was lying flat on her back with a bad back. I don't think she could have gotten through it if she had not been in a captive position. (This book is version seventeen and lovingly called "Short and Sweet.")

Thank you to my birthday club friends (Jenny, Sue, Lola and Kathy), each interesting and unique women in good marriages. My friends stood by me when I was having some of my most difficult marital times. Good friends are one of the richest resources of our lives.

Thank you to my soul friend Ursula. You listened to me, encouraged me to graph my thoughts, and have been a constant sounding board.

Thank you to Jim and Bernard. You gave me the basis for recognizing an enriching relationship and knowing that they do exist.

Thank you to my daughter Jena for putting up with ten years of hearing about "the book." Jena, it's finally here. Thank you for being the best daughter a mother could have. You will also be one of the best partners anyone could have after listening to your mother all these years!

And finally, Melinda... We have had someone looking over us to put us together over the last eighteen years, just when we needed each other. This book never could have come together without all of your help.

SURVEY FOR OUR READERS

We want your opinion!

We encourage you to complete the survey about *Relationship Rights (and wrongs)* on the next page. The results will be used to further develop the concept of this book from the viewpoint of people like you. We welcome any comments you feel are appropriate to include on additional pages. All of the information will be kept in the strictest confidence. You will remain anonymous unless you specify differently.

Please return the following survey to us at the address below.

We would appreciate any comments or input you might have. Thank you in advance for your help!

Relationship Rights (and wrongs)
10936 N. Port Washington #269
Mequon, WI 53092
fax: 262-242-7639
e-mail: *feedback@relationshiprights.com*

***You may also visit us on our website at:* www.relationshiprights.com.**

Relationship Rights (and wrongs) Survey

1) Did you find *Relationship Rights (and wrongs)* helpful?

    ___ Yes   ___ No   Why? _____

    _____

    _____

2) Which relationship rights were most applicable to you and your relationship? Please list.

    _____

    _____

    _____

3) To what degree did you find the following parts of the book helpful?

	Not helpful				Very helpful

Part One—Relationship Guide

	Not helpful				Very helpful
___ Green Rights	1	2	3	4	5
___ Yellow Rights	1	2	3	4	5
___ Red Rights	1	2	3	4	5
___ Reality Bites (personal examples)	1	2	3	4	5
___ Definitions of Rights	1	2	3	4	5

Part Two—Relationship Reality Check

___ Relationship Scales	1	2	3	4	5
___ Calculations for Relationship Scales	1	2	3	4	5
___ How Far Is Too Far?	1	2	3	4	5
___ Journaling Activities	1	2	3	4	5
___ Remember, Relationships Work Two Ways	1	2	3	4	5

4) How were you feeling about your relationship before you read the book?

___ good   ___ okay   ___ unhappy

___ confused   ___ afraid   ___ hard to describe

___ I'd like to explain _____

_____

5) Did the book help you? ___ Yes ___ No   If yes, how did it help? (check all that apply)

___ to recognize where I was in the relationship

___ to understand my feelings about the relationship

___ to give me the language to express my feelings and concerns

___ to show what can be done to improve the relationship

___ to help validate my leaving the relationship

___ to help communicate with my partner

___ to improve my behavior toward my partner

___ to help express myself to my therapist/counselor

___ other _____

_____

6) How did you use this book (check all that apply):?

___ by myself   ___ with my partner   ___ with a therapist

___ with my child   ___ with a friend   ___ in a support group

___ other (please specify) _____

7) Would you recommend it to others? Who and why? ___ yes ___ no

_____

_____

_____

8) Did you make decisions about yourself or changes in your relationship after reading this book? ___ yes ___ no

If yes, would you share what they were and are you happier now as a result of them? (You may add more lines or paper).

_____

_____

_____

9) Do you think you will continue to use or refer to *Relationship Rights (and wrongs)* in the future? ___ yes ___ no

If yes, how (check all that apply)?

___ I will keep it on my bookshelf but probably won't read it again.

___ I will keep it on my bookshelf and may refer to it from time to time.

___ I will probably use it in the future to help me clarify things when I'm feeling confused.

___ I will ask my partner to read it.

___ I will use it in my/our therapy sessions.

___ I will give it to a friend.

___ I will save it to give to my daughter or son to read when I feel the time is appropriate.

___ Other (please specify): _____

_____

_____

10) Other comments and suggestions (add additional pages if necessary):

_____

_____

Other Offerings

If the following were offered for *Relationship Rights (and wrongs)*, would you participate (check all that apply)?

___ Seminars	___ Workbooks
___ Counseling sessions	___ Tapes
___ Support groups in your hometown	___ Anonymous teleconference groups
___ On-line support groups	___ Other recommendations

If yes to the above, how do you see yourself participating?

___ as a couple	___ by myself
___ with friends	___ as a facilitator

About Yourself

I AM: ___ female ___ male

I AM: ___ under 20 ___ 20-25 ___ 26-35 ___ 36-45 ___ 46-55 ___ 55+

Current Relationship Status:

___ married (to first spouse) ___ separated ___ divorced

___ remarried ___ live with partner ___ single

___ widowed

How would you describe your current relationship?

___ Happy together ___ Unhappy, but together

___ Not perfect, but okay ___ Abused but together

___ Confused, but together ___ Separated or divorced

How did you hear about the book (check all that apply)?

___ book review ___ store display ___ Internet

___ advertisement ___ article ___ word of mouth

___ professional referral ___ heard authors ___ other

___ radio talk show (specify) ————————————————

___ TV talk show (specify) ————————————————

Where did you buy this book?

___ bookstore ___ radio/TV (specify)

___ our website ___ other website (specify)

___ seminar ___ book club

___ heard the authors speak ___ given to me

___ other ___ professional office or organization

Your occupation: —————— Partner's occupation: ——————

Total household income (optional):

___ <$25,000 ___ $25,000-$49,999 ___ $50,000-100,000 ___ > $100,000

REQUEST FORM FOR MORE INFORMATION OR FOR ORDERING

(Please feel free to duplicate this form.)

Please send me more information about:

___ future publications or products   ___ support groups

___ seminars   ___ Internet chat room

___ Add me to your mailing list   ___ Send me e-mail updates

___ My e-mail address is: _____

___ I have filled out my address in the order section below.

I would like to order ___ copies of Relationship Rights (and wrongs)

___ Book(s) (@ $16.00 ea.) $_____

___ Workbook(s) ($15.00 ea) $_____

___ Tape of workshop ($9.00 ea) $_____

Sales Tax
(Wisconsin residents add 5.6%) $_____

Shipping and Handling
($3.95 for first item, $1.00 for each additional item) $_____

Total Amount Enclosed $_____
(Prices effective January 1, 2004. Future prices are subject to change.)

Ordered by: **Ship to (if different from ordered by):**

Name: _____   Name: _____

Address:_____   Address:_____

City_____   City: _____

State: _____ Zip: _____   State: _____ Zip: _____

Day Phone: _____   Day Phone: _____

Type of Payment: ___ check/money order *(made payable to Checkpoint Publishing)*

    ___ credit card   Master Card/Visa Card number:

___ ___ ___ ___ - ___ ___ ___ ___ - ___ ___ ___ ___ - ___ ___ ___ ___   Expiration Date: ___ / ___

Your signature:_____

Print name as it appears on card: _____

Mail your order to:

Checkpoint Publishing c/o Champion Press Ltd.
4308 Blueberry Road
Fredonia, Wisconsin 53021